THE
ULTIMATE
EGGHEADS
QUIZ BOOK

THE ULTIMATE EGGHEADS QUIZ BOOK

SIMON & SCHUSTER

London · New York · Sydney · Toronto · New Delhi

A CBS COMPANY

First published in Great Britain by Simon & Schuster UK Ltd, 2013
A CBS COMPANY

Copyright © 2013, 12 Yard Productions

1 3 5 7 9 10 8 6 4 2

Simon & Schuster UK Ltd
1st Floor
222 Gray's Inn Road
London WC1X 8HB

www.simonandschuster.co.uk

Simon & Schuster Australia, Sydney
Simon & Schuster India, New Delhi

The author and publishers have made all reasonable
efforts to contact copyright-holders for permission, and apologise
for any omissions or errors in the form of credits given.
Corrections may be made to future printings.

A CIP catalogue record for this book is available
from the British Library

ISBN: 978-1-47113-155-4
eBook ISBN: 978-1-47113-156-1

Typeset in the UK by M Rules
Printed and bound by CPI Group (UK) Ltd, Croydon, CR0 4YY

CONTENTS

INTRODUCTION

It's hard to believe it's been ten years.

What started as a rather quirky daytime parlour game with just a five week run on BBC1 in 2003, has quietly become part of the quiz establishment. During that decade we've made hundreds of shows (well over a thousand in fact) and asked tens of thousands of questions. And, of course, we've given away more than a million pounds – a significant chunk of that in one of the most dramatic episodes ever, when a team of students scooped a mighty £75,000 in one go, after the Eggheads had gone fifteen straight weeks without a loss. The final question on the death penalty in the United States (Killer Question 2, in this book) remains etched in my memory – I was terrified when I asked it. I can only imagine how the students felt when the Eggheads got it wrong.

The Eggheads themselves never cease to amaze me, their dedication and sheer will to win every single contest shows no sign of diminishing – in fact quite the opposite. I often wonder if they could play on their own chosen categories, would they ever lose? What Chris doesn't know about steam engines could be written on a stamp with a whitewash brush; Daphne, quietly enticing opponents to take her on at sport; Barry's amazing knowledge of 1970s prog rock; Dave on Manchester United; Pat on animated films; Judith on the royal family (only joking Judith!); And Kevin on . . . well anything apart from food and drink . . .

Dermot Murnaghan, 2013

Since we are talking *Eggheads*, I'll start with a question.

What exactly is CJ de Mooi made of?

It was a single conversation with him that made me realise quizzers are, quite simply, built from different material.

He had just raised himself from one of the rickety plastic chairs we keep firmly hidden from view while filming *Eggheads*. The contest was over, the contestants were filing out of the studio, the filaments were fading in the lighting rig above us and I was making small talk.

'You're very good on your movies, CJ,' I said. He had just won a Film & TV round.

'Thanks,' he replied. He is nothing if not succinct.

'I mean, if I just threw a movie title at you I bet you'd know all about it.'

'Might do.'

'Okay,' I said, not thinking that I was initiating the kind of conversation the Eggheads face every time they are recognised in the street, 'What about – *Tootsie*?

'What about it?'

'Year?'

'1982.'

'Director?'

'Sydney Pollack.'

'Any Oscars?'

'Only Jessica Lange,' he told me, 'for best actress in a supporting role.'

'What about Oscar nominations?'

'Nine.'

'Nine. Who wrote it?'

'Larry Gelbart.'

By this stage I was overwhelmed by facts, so I asked CJ: 'And what did you think of *Tootsie*?'

'I don't know,' he replied. 'I've never seen it.'

In that one sentence CJ showed why he, and the others who like to know stuff for the sake of knowing stuff, are built differently. CJ has his passions, sure – tennis and chess come to mind, as well as walking around with no shirt on. But the gaps will be filled in by sheer hard work. The Eggheads do not know about *Tootsie* because the knowledge happened to come to them, as it does for most of us; they know about *Tootsie* because they hunted those facts down like trained assassins.

Which is why they're wonderful. And adorable. And very slightly bonkers.

It's why every visiting quizzer in every team that passes through our studio longs to beat them.

And why I, very secretly, desperately want them to.

Jeremy Vine, 2013

EGGHEADS: THE PROGRAMME

Every day on *Eggheads* a new team of challengers pit their quizzing know-how against arguably Britain's toughest quiz team – The Eggheads.

Teams of five challengers go up against the Eggheads in four head-to-head rounds. If they win a head-to-head then it guarantees them an extra player in the all-important final general knowledge round. This is where the money is won or lost. Lose a head-to-head however and the Egghead will instead be in the final.

The four head-to-head rounds are drawn from the following nine subjects: history, sport, politics, science, music, food & drink, film & television, geography and arts & books.

Each day £1,000 is up for grabs; however, if the challengers fail to win then the money rolls over to the next show.

The History of *Eggheads*

Eggheads first appeared on our screens on 10 November 2003 when a team called the Motormen challenged our quiz goliaths. Since then over 1200 episodes have been filmed and over 40,000 questions have been asked.

The first team to beat the Eggheads were called The Unicorn and they won £13,000. By our 1000th episode, broadcast on 18 May 2012, only 82 teams had beaten the Eggheads.

The biggest prize fund won to date was £75,000 by a team of students called Beer Today Gone Tomorrow.

Up to episode 1000 there had only been seven occasions when there has been just one Egghead left in the final. Of those seven occasions there has only been one when the Eggheads lost – that was Kevin playing against the Cartoonists in October 2009.

As of episode 1000 Pat, Barry and Kevin had never lost at history, and Kevin hasn't ever got a history question wrong in a head to head.

In 1000 episodes only nine teams have managed to beat the Eggheads with only one player in the final round.

HOW TO PLAY *EGGHEADS*
USING THIS BOOK

For a complete game of *Eggheads* using *The Ultimate Eggheads Quiz Book*, you will need:

- *2 teams with 5 players on each team*
- *A Question Master who is not part of either team*

Before starting, decide which team will be the **Challengers** and which team will be the **Eggheads**, and appoint someone impartial to take the role of Question Master who will be responsible for picking the category for each of the first four rounds and asking the questions.

Played in five rounds: the first four rounds are each based on a different category (specialist subject), and the final round is made up of general knowledge questions.

In each of these first four rounds, the **Challengers** are given a category by the Question Master and must choose a member of their own team to play, and a member of the **Eggheads** against whom they wish to compete.

The challenger is given the choice of going first or second, and both players are then asked in turn three questions each, which have multiple choice answers.

Example:

1. Opened in 1932, the famous theatre called the Radio City Music Hall is in which city in the United States?
   - ⌴ Los Angeles
   - ⌴ New York
   - ⌴ New Orleans

<u>**The players chosen for these first four rounds must not confer with their team members on their answers.**</u>

The round continues until each competitor has been asked their three specialist subject questions by the Question Master. If after three questions each there is no winner (i.e. players have answered an equal amount of questions right or wrong), the round then goes into sudden death with the Question Master asking each player a question from the same category but giving no multiple choice answers.

Example:

2. 'Earth stood hard as iron' is a line in the first verse of which Christmas carol?

The player who wins their specialist subject round is then eligible to play for their team in the final general knowledge round, whilst the losing players are not allowed to participate in this final round.

The general knowledge round is played in exactly the same format as the head-to-head rounds – three questions each with sudden death should there be a draw – and questions can be drawn from any of the general knowledge sections in the book. The winning team is decided on this final round.

Good Luck!

DAPHNE FOWLER

FULL NAME:
Daphne Ann Fowler

HOME TOWN:
Weston-super-Mare

EDUCATION:
Folkestone Girls Grammar School 1950–7: 7 O-levels, 2 A-levels.
Exeter University 1957–9: two years of a Theology degree; left before
completion.

QUIZZING CREDENTIALS:
Brain of Britain 1997 (last lady to win it), *Fifteen to One*, series
champion twice, and winner of the top of the finals board trophy 3
times (2000–2002). I won the car on *Sale of the Century* in 1983 and
was England's representative on the Australian version of *Sale of the
Century* (1986, 1987 and 1988.)

LEAST FAVOURITE SUBJECT:
Sport

SPECIAL INTEREST:
Any aspect of general knowledge. I've loved reading encyclopedias and dictionaries ever since I was a child.

HOBBIES:
Reading, more reading, and my family, especially my great-grandchildren.

WHAT DOES IT TAKE TO BE AN EGGHEAD:
All round good general knowledge, plus the ability, when you don't know the answer for sure, to be able to work out logically what the right answer should be out of the three options given.

WHO WOULD BE ON YOUR ULTIMATE FANTASY QUIZ TEAM:
Irene Thomas, the second lady to win *Brain of Britain* in 1961, who inspired me, Jesse Honey, a recent winner of *Mastermind*, because he's young and has won the World Championship, Kevin, Pat, Barry (of course!) and me.

MOST MEMORABLE MOMENT DURING YOUR TIME AS AN EGGHEAD:
Twice having to face the contestants on my own and winning both times!

WHAT ADVICE DO YOU HAVE FOR ANY BUDDING EGGHEADS:
Enter as many quizzes as you can, read the newspaper thoroughly every day, and if you do become an Egghead, have fun just as I have had.

WHAT IS YOUR FAVOURITE FACT OR PIECE OF TRIVIA:
Too many to single one out, but how about the typographical '@' sign, which is called an 'arobase'. I love unusual and obscure words which apparently makes me a 'sequipedalian'. One of my favourite books is *Mrs Byrne's Dictionary of Unusual, Obscure and Preposterous Words*, which contains so many 'I didn't know that' words, such as a 'philocubist', which means a lover of dice games.

LITTLE KNOWN FACT ABOUT YOU:
I won my first car in 1969 when I wrote a winning slogan for Energen crispbreads: 'I buy Energen crispbreads because "it's so easy to choose, you've got nothing to lose, but your weight!"'

1. What was the name of the group who had a UK hit single in 1981 with 'The Birdie Song'?
   - ⊔ The Twitters
   - ⊔ The Tweets
   - ⊔ The Tweedles

2. In Gustav Holst's suite *The Planets* which planet is described as the 'Bringer of War'?
   - ⊔ Venus
   - ⊔ Saturn
   - ⊔ Mars

3. Who wrote the music for the 1902 operetta *Merrie England*?
   - ⊔ Edward German
   - ⊔ John Ireland
   - ⊔ Benjamin Britten

4. 'Oh Carol' and 'Happy Birthday Sweet Sixteen' were the biggest UK hit singles for which singer?
   - ⊔ Bobby Darin
   - ⊔ Gene Pitney
   - ⊔ Neil Sedaka

5. The American Carl Stalling, born in 1891, is best known as a composer of what?
   - ⊔ National Anthems
   - ⊔ Cartoon Music
   - ⊔ TV Commercial Jingles

6. 'The Piano Sonata No. 21 in C Major Opus 53', also known as the 'Waldstein Sonata', is a work by which composer?
   - ⊔ Beethoven
   - ⊔ Bach
   - ⊔ Mozart

ANSWERS ON P.271

7. What name is given to a group of musical notes sounded together, as a basis of harmony?
   - ⌣ Chord
   - ⌣ Scale
   - ⌣ Fret

8. What is the term for a loudspeaker that reproduces high frequencies?
   - ⌣ Subwoofer
   - ⌣ Woofer
   - ⌣ Tweeter

9. John Entwistle was the bassist with which highly successful band?
   - ⌣ The Who
   - ⌣ The Doors
   - ⌣ The Animals

10. The US band leader Benny Goodman was best known for playing which musical instrument?
   - ⌣ Saxophone
   - ⌣ Clarinet
   - ⌣ Trumpet

11. What name is given to the area of a theatre where the orchestra is located?
   - ⌣ Cave
   - ⌣ Crater
   - ⌣ Pit

12. The Yorkshireman John Barry is particularly well-known for composing what type of music?
   - ⌣ Opera
   - ⌣ Film Scores
   - ⌣ Hymns

ANSWERS ON P.271

13. What name is given to large overnight dance parties, especially those laid on during the late 1980s and early 1990s?
    ⊔ Rants
    ⊔ Raves
    ⊔ Roars

14. In the song 'Do-Re-Mi' from the musical *The Sound of Music*, the note 're' is described as 'a drop of golden' what?
    ⊔ Syrup
    ⊔ Sand
    ⊔ Sun

15. Puccini's opera *La Bohème* is set in which city?
    ⊔ Paris
    ⊔ Rome
    ⊔ Madrid

16. 'The Club Is Alive' was a UK number one single for which pop group in July 2010?
    ⊔ Black Eyed Peas
    ⊔ N-Dubz
    ⊔ JLS

17. Who sang the theme song to the Bruce Willis/Cybill Shepherd TV series *Moonlighting*?
    ⊔ George Benson
    ⊔ James Ingram
    ⊔ Al Jarreau

18. 'Crazy' was a top ten hit single in America for which singer?
    ⊔ Patsy Cline
    ⊔ Loretta Lynn
    ⊔ Tammy Wynette

ANSWERS ON P.271

19. In which decade were 'Hit Me With Your Rhythm Stick' and 'Tie A Yellow Ribbon Round The Ole Oak Tree' UK number one singles?
    ⊔ 1970s
    ⊔ 1980s
    ⊔ 1990s

20. The French jazz musician Stéphane Grappelli was famous for playing which instrument?
    ⊔ Drums
    ⊔ Saxophone
    ⊔ Violin

21. Which musical features the songs 'It Couldn't Please Me More' and 'Don't Tell Mama'?
    ⊔ The Sound of Music
    ⊔ Cabaret
    ⊔ Singin' In The Rain

22. *Fear of Music*, *More Songs about Buildings and Food* and *Little Creatures* were top 40 albums for which American band?
    ⊔ Talking Heads
    ⊔ Metallica
    ⊔ The Stooges

23. 'Day-o, day-o/ Daylight come and me wan' go home' are the opening lines to which song?
    ⊔ Mary's Boy Child
    ⊔ The Banana Boat Song
    ⊔ Island In The Sun

24. 'You Really Got Me' was a UK hit single in 1964 for which band?
    ⊔ The Kinks
    ⊔ Manfred Mann
    ⊔ The Yardbirds

ANSWERS ON P.271

25. By what name is the singer born Graham McPherson better known?
- ⊔ Elvis Costello
- ⊔ Adam Ant
- ⊔ Suggs

26. In the musical *The Sound of Music*, what is the name of the youngest child of Georg Von Trapp?
- ⊔ Marta
- ⊔ Gretl
- ⊔ Louisa

27. What name is given to the melody pipe on a set of bagpipes?
- ⊔ Chanter
- ⊔ Bagad
- ⊔ Stock

28. 'Suedehead', released in 1988, was the first solo single to enter the UK charts for which male vocalist?
- ⊔ Morrissey
- ⊔ Sting
- ⊔ Paul Weller

29. Which comic opera by Gilbert and Sullivan is subtitled 'The Lass That Loved a Sailor'?
- ⊔ The Mikado
- ⊔ The Pirates of Penzance
- ⊔ HMS Pinafore

30. 'And now, the end is near; And so I face the final curtain' is the first line of which well-known song?
- ⊔ Light My Fire
- ⊔ Magic Moments
- ⊔ My Way

ANSWERS ON P.271

31. 'The Invitation to the Jellicle Ball' and 'The Rum Tum Tugger' are songs from which Andrew Lloyd Webber musical?
- ⊔ Sunset Boulevard
- ⊔ Cats
- ⊔ Evita

32. After leaving the Specials, Terry Hall became the lead singer of which band?
- ⊔ UB40
- ⊔ Haircut 100
- ⊔ Fun Boy Three

33. Which band's single 'Whole Lotta Love' was used, in many forms, for many years as the theme tune for the TV show *Top of the Pops*?
- ⊔ Led Zeppelin
- ⊔ The Rolling Stones
- ⊔ The Beatles

34. The 'Psalms' composed by Leonard Bernstein in 1965 were written for which cathedral?
- ⊔ Chichester
- ⊔ Cologne
- ⊔ Chartres

35. What is the name of the central male character in the stage musical *We Will Rock You*?
- ⊔ Galileo
- ⊔ Fandango
- ⊔ Beelzebub

36. What is the title of the Beatles song that begins 'I once had a girl, or should I say, she once had me ...'?
- ⊔ Maxwell's Silver Hammer
- ⊔ Nowhere Man
- ⊔ Norwegian Wood

ANSWERS ON P.271

37. The 1984 film *Purple Rain* starred and featured music by which singer?
- ⊔ Madonna
- ⊔ Michael Jackson
- ⊔ Prince

38. Gene Simmons is a founder member of which US rock band, known for wearing black and white make-up?
- ⊔ Kiss
- ⊔ Guns N' Roses
- ⊔ Bon Jovi

39. What type of musical instrument is the Indian 'tabla'?
- ⊔ Percussion
- ⊔ String
- ⊔ Wind

40. Simian Records is the name of a music label founded by which *Lord of the Rings* actor?
- ⊔ Sean Bean
- ⊔ Elijah Wood
- ⊔ Orlando Bloom

41. Which singer did Orson Welles once call 'the most exciting woman in the world'?
- ⊔ Shirley Bassey
- ⊔ Marlene Dietrich
- ⊔ Eartha Kitt

42. Which Scandinavian country opened its first opera house in 2008?
- ⊔ Norway
- ⊔ Denmark
- ⊔ Sweden

ANSWERS ON P.271

43. 'We've taken to you so strong, it's clear we're going to get along' are lines from which song in the musical *Oliver!*?
   ⌞⌟ Boy for Sale
   ⌞⌟ Food Glorious Food
   ⌞⌟ Consider Yourself

44. 'Sailing' was a UK number one single for Rod Stewart in which year?
   ⌞⌟ 1965
   ⌞⌟ 1975
   ⌞⌟ 1985

45. 'Kinky Afro', 'Loose Fit' and 'Step On' were UK hit singles in the early 1990s for which Manchester band?
   ⌞⌟ Stone Roses
   ⌞⌟ Charlatans
   ⌞⌟ Happy Mondays

46. The tune to 'Land Of Hope And Glory' was taken from part of which of Edward Elgar's works?
   ⌞⌟ Pomp and Circumstance
   ⌞⌟ Enigma Variations
   ⌞⌟ In the South

47. What nationality was Bizet, the composer of the operas *Carmen* and *The Pearl Fishers*?
   ⌞⌟ French
   ⌞⌟ Italian
   ⌞⌟ German

48. What name is given to the style of close harmony unaccompanied singing usually performed by four males?
   ⌞⌟ Boatshed
   ⌞⌟ Boardwalk
   ⌞⌟ Barbershop

ANSWERS ON P.271

49. Which Irving Berlin song begins with the line 'Heaven, I'm in Heaven'?
- ⌣ Hand In Hand
- ⌣ Side By Side
- ⌣ Cheek To Cheek

50. Who was the lead singer of 1980s groups the Communards and Bronski Beat?
- ⌣ Boy George
- ⌣ Jimmy Somerville
- ⌣ Paul Weller

51. What item is mentioned in the first line of the Christmas carol known as 'Deck the Halls'?
- ⌣ Boughs of Holly
- ⌣ Sprigs of Mistletoe
- ⌣ Ribbons of Gold

52. 'Nothing's Gonna Stop Us Now' was a UK number one hit single in 1987 for which band?
- ⌣ Europe
- ⌣ Starship
- ⌣ Bon Jovi

53. The American singer Tammy Wynette was known as 'The First Lady . . .' of what?
- ⌣ Country Music
- ⌣ Soul Music
- ⌣ Rock Music

54. Which singer co-wrote Kylie Minogue's UK number one hit single 'Can't Get You Out Of My Head' with Rob Davis?
- ⌣ Hazell Dean
- ⌣ Betty Boo
- ⌣ Cathy Dennis

ANSWERS ON P.271

55. *Autobahn* is the title of a 1970s album by which band?
- ⌣ Nena
- ⌣ Kraftwerk
- ⌣ Sparks

56. *Sketches of Spain* is a celebrated album by which jazz musician?
- ⌣ Charlie Parker
- ⌣ Miles Davis
- ⌣ Chet Baker

57. Vince Neil, John Corabi, Tommy Lee, Mick Mars and Nikki Sixx have all been members of which heavy metal band?
- ⌣ Hanoi Rocks
- ⌣ Mötley Crüe
- ⌣ W.A.S.P.

58. Which band formed in the wake of the demise of Joy Division?
- ⌣ New Order
- ⌣ New Model Army
- ⌣ New Edition

59. What was the title of the 1982 UK top ten hit single for Joan Jett and the Blackhearts?
- ⌣ I Love R 'n' B
- ⌣ I Love Rock 'n' Roll
- ⌣ I Love Opera

60. With which instrument is young classical musician Nicola Benedetti most associated?
- ⌣ Cello
- ⌣ Harp
- ⌣ Violin

ANSWERS ON P.271

61. In 1995, what was the title of the first UK number one hit single for Oasis?
   ⊔ Some Might Say
   ⊔ Roll With It
   ⊔ Wonderwall

62. *The Coronation of Poppea* was the last completed opera of which composer?
   ⊔ Domenico Scarlatti
   ⊔ Claudio Monteverdi
   ⊔ Henry Purcell

63. 'Common time' in musical notation is a time signature indicating how many beats to the bar?
   ⊔ One
   ⊔ Four
   ⊔ Ten

64. Which group sang with Fun Boy Three on the 1982 UK hit single 'It Ain't What You Do It's The Way That You Do It'?
   ⊔ Bucks Fizz
   ⊔ Culture Club
   ⊔ Bananarama

65. 'Union Of The Snake' was a 1983 UK top 10 hit single for which band?
   ⊔ Human League
   ⊔ Duran Duran
   ⊔ Spandau Ballet

66. Which term refers to the expressive fluctuation of speed within a musical piece?
   ⊔ Rubato
   ⊔ Obbligato
   ⊔ Intermezzo

ANSWERS ON P.271

67. Which band released the albums *Beggars Banquet* and *Exile on Main Street*?
⊔ The Rolling Stones
⊔ The Grateful Dead
⊔ The Who

68. 'Confide In Me' and 'Spinning Around' were UK hit singles for which singer?
⊔ Madonna
⊔ Britney Spears
⊔ Kylie Minogue

69. What is the name of the preacher's son in the Dusty Springfield song 'Son Of A Preacher Man'?
⊔ Johnny-James
⊔ Billy-Ray
⊔ Frankie-Lee

70. What is the term for a melody played in conjunction with another, a technique used in the Irving Berlin song 'You're Just In Love'?
⊔ Modulation
⊔ Descant
⊔ Counterpoint

71. Who composed the opera *Lady Macbeth of the Mtsensk District*?
⊔ Shostakovich
⊔ Tchaikovsky
⊔ Stravinsky

72. Which be-bop artist is credited with writing the jazz standard 'Salt Peanuts'?
⊔ Charlie Parker
⊔ Dizzy Gillespie
⊔ John Coltrane

ANSWERS ON P.271

73. What was the name of the Spice Girls' debut single which topped the UK charts in 1996?
- ⊔ C'est La Vie
- ⊔ Wannabe
- ⊔ Sound Of The Underground

74. 'Raindrops on roses and whiskers on kittens' is the first line of a song from which musical?
- ⊔ Mary Poppins
- ⊔ The Sound of Music
- ⊔ Guys and Dolls

75. Which artist wrote the song 'Knockin' On Heaven's Door' in 1973?
- ⊔ Bob Dylan
- ⊔ Bob Marley
- ⊔ Robert Plant

76. 'Nobody's Diary' and 'Don't Go' were UK hit singles in the 1980s for which duo?
- ⊔ Pet Shop Boys
- ⊔ Dollar
- ⊔ Yazoo

77. Which character did Michael Jackson play in the 1978 film *The Wiz*?
- ⊔ Tinman
- ⊔ Lion
- ⊔ Scarecrow

78. *Oberto, Conte di San Bonifacio*, premiered in 1839, is an opera by which composer?
- ⊔ Rossini
- ⊔ Verdi
- ⊔ Vivaldi

ANSWERS ON P.271

79. Which tempo marking in music is derived from the Italian for 'at ease'?
- ⌴ Andante
- ⌴ Adagio
- ⌴ Allegro

80. The Hallé Orchestra is based in which British city?
- ⌴ Edinburgh
- ⌴ Manchester
- ⌴ Cardiff

81. Before he took up the trumpet, Louis Armstrong was a professional musician on which instrument?
- ⌴ Guitar
- ⌴ Cornet
- ⌴ Flute

82. The form of vocal chamber music known as the 'madrigal' originated during the 14th century in which country?
- ⌴ Germany
- ⌴ France
- ⌴ Italy

83. The violinist Nigel Kennedy was born in which year?
- ⌴ 1956
- ⌴ 1966
- ⌴ 1976

84. What name was given to a type of musical ensemble associated with playing jazz music popular in the 1920s and 1930s?
- ⌴ Big Band
- ⌴ Brass Band
- ⌴ Boy Band

ANSWERS ON P.271

85. *Pacific Ocean Blue* is the title of the only solo album by which of the original Beach Boys line-up?
    ⊔ Carl Wilson
    ⊔ Dennis Wilson
    ⊔ Brian Wilson

86. Who composed the comic opera *Der Rosenkavalier*?
    ⊔ Richard Strauss
    ⊔ Richard Wagner
    ⊔ Jacques Offenbach

87. What name is given to the Southern US offshoot of rap music that features repetitive rhythms and chants?
    ⊔ Crunk
    ⊔ Boink
    ⊔ Grind

88. Which musical instrument would be classed as an idiophone?
    ⊔ Piano
    ⊔ Xylophone
    ⊔ Cello

89. Which character sings the song 'Some Day My Prince Will Come' in a Disney animated film?
    ⊔ Snow White
    ⊔ Cinderella
    ⊔ The Little Mermaid

90. Which heavy metal band had a UK number one album called *Back in Black*?
    ⊔ Metallica
    ⊔ Deep Purple
    ⊔ AC/DC

ANSWERS ON P.271

91. The jazz pioneer Max Roach is best known for his skill on which instrument?
- ⊔ Drums
- ⊔ Piano
- ⊔ Trumpet

92. Who released the 1968 album known as *The Village Green Preservation Society*?
- ⊔ Donovan
- ⊔ The Kinks
- ⊔ Pink Floyd

93. 'Walkin' Back To Happiness' was a UK number one hit single in 1961 for which singer?
- ⊔ Helen Shapiro
- ⊔ Petula Clark
- ⊔ Lulu

94. A famous music-hall song, written by Fred Gilbert tells of the newly acquired status and manner of 'The Man Who Broke The Bank ...' where?
- ⊔ On Piccadilly
- ⊔ At Monte Carlo
- ⊔ In Dublin City

95. Which member of Girls Aloud was born in Northern Ireland?
- ⊔ Nicola Roberts
- ⊔ Nadine Coyle
- ⊔ Kimberley Walsh

96. A musical chord made up of three notes – the root, the third and the fifth – is known as what?
- ⊔ Tripos
- ⊔ Triad
- ⊔ Trigram

ANSWERS ON P.271

97. What was the first name of the Russian composer Stravinsky?
    ⊐ Igor
    ⊐ Alexander
    ⊐ Leo

98. The UK hit singles 'Child' and 'Clementine' and the album *Green Man* were solo projects by which member of Take That?
    ⊐ Howard Donald
    ⊐ Jason Orange
    ⊐ Mark Owen

99. How many strings does a standard double bass have?
    ⊐ 4
    ⊐ 6
    ⊐ 8

100. In which year was Charlotte Church born?
    ⊐ 1976
    ⊐ 1981
    ⊐ 1986

ANSWERS ON P.271

1. **Which hairstyle for men shares its name with a type of fish?**
   - ⌐ Kipper
   - ⌐ Trout
   - ⌐ Mullet

2. **Which type of dog has varieties known as 'flat-coated', 'curly coated' and 'golden'?**
   - ⌐ Spaniel
   - ⌐ Retriever
   - ⌐ Setter

3. **If someone is born on Christmas Day, what is their star sign?**
   - ⌐ Virgo
   - ⌐ Capricorn
   - ⌐ Leo

4. **In the original arcade game, what type of creature was 'Donkey Kong'?**
   - ⌐ Mule
   - ⌐ Gorilla
   - ⌐ Hedgehog

5. **The International Court of Justice is based in which European city?**
   - ⌐ Strasbourg
   - ⌐ The Hague
   - ⌐ Brussels

6. **Who played the amateur witch Eglantine Price in the 1971 film *Bedknobs and Broomsticks*?**
   - ⌐ Angela Lansbury
   - ⌐ Julie Andrews
   - ⌐ Maggie Smith

ANSWERS ON P.272

7. 1 Carlton Gardens is the official ministerial residence of which member of the Cabinet?
   - ⊔ Chancellor
   - ⊔ Foreign Secretary
   - ⊔ Transport Secretary

8. Who succeeded Brezhnev as General Secretary of the Communist Party of the Soviet Union in November 1982?
   - ⊔ Andropov
   - ⊔ Gorbachev
   - ⊔ Khrushchev

9. Matt, Luke and Craig were members of which 1980s boy band?
   - ⊔ Haircut 100
   - ⊔ Duran Duran
   - ⊔ Bros

10. In a standard game of Scrabble, each player starts a game with how many tiles?
    - ⊔ 7
    - ⊔ 10
    - ⊔ 13

11. What collective noun is used for a group of rhino?
    - ⊔ Crash
    - ⊔ Bang
    - ⊔ Wallop

12. Orvieto is a light white wine from which country?
    - ⊔ Italy
    - ⊔ France
    - ⊔ Spain

ANSWERS ON P.272

13. The TV personality of the 1950s and 1960s, Sir Mortimer Wheeler, was an expert in which field?
- ⌙ Ballet
- ⌙ Food and Drink
- ⌙ Archaeology

14. The French national theatre awards are named after which playwright?
- ⌙ Molière
- ⌙ Racine
- ⌙ Corneille

15. What has been the official home of the Archbishop of Canterbury since 1197?
- ⌙ Somerset House
- ⌙ Hampton Court
- ⌙ Lambeth Palace

16. In which year did Erno Rubik invent his 'Magic Cube' that was later sold as the Rubik's Cube?
- ⌙ 1954
- ⌙ 1964
- ⌙ 1974

17. The Prairie Wolf is another name for which animal?
- ⌙ Ocelot
- ⌙ Vicuna
- ⌙ Coyote

18. The island called Vulcano is just off the northern coast of which larger island?
- ⌙ Sicily
- ⌙ Iceland
- ⌙ Sumatra

ANSWERS ON P.272

19. According to legend, which creatures saved the city of Rome from besieging Gauls in 390 BC?
- ⊔ Dogs
- ⊔ Geese
- ⊔ Owls

20. Bjorn and which other man were the male members of the group ABBA?
- ⊔ Benny
- ⊔ Barry
- ⊔ Bono

21. What is a 'Singapore Sling'?
- ⊔ A Dance
- ⊔ A Hairstyle
- ⊔ A Cocktail

22. The Hanging Gardens of Babylon were watered by pumps from which river?
- ⊔ Nile
- ⊔ Euphrates
- ⊔ Tigris

23. In which decade was VAT first introduced in Britain?
- ⊔ 1920s
- ⊔ 1940s
- ⊔ 1970s

24. What is the smallest of the four main islands that comprise Japan?
- ⊔ Shikoku
- ⊔ Kyushu
- ⊔ Hokkaido

ANSWERS ON P.272

25. In Hinduism, the semi-divine being known as 'Hanuman' takes the form of which creature?
- ⌣ Elephant
- ⌣ Tiger
- ⌣ Monkey

26. Which area of the United States was hit by devastating wildfires in 2007?
- ⌣ Virginia
- ⌣ Hawaii
- ⌣ California

27. What word is used for a pair of something, especially birds or mammals killed in hunting?
- ⌣ Brace
- ⌣ Collar
- ⌣ Tie

28. Cape Horn is the southernmost point of which continent?
- ⌣ Africa
- ⌣ South America
- ⌣ Antarctica

29. What sort of food would you buy in a French boulangerie?
- ⌣ Bread
- ⌣ Meat
- ⌣ Cheese

30. What is the name of the character played by Lee Marvin in the 1967 thriller *Point Blank*?
- ⌣ Hickman
- ⌣ Walker
- ⌣ Reisman

ANSWERS ON P.272

31. The London street Savile Row is synonymous with which profession?
- ⊔ Banking
- ⊔ Tailoring
- ⊔ Acting

32. The term 'Nubia' refers to an ancient region on which continent?
- ⊔ Asia
- ⊔ Africa
- ⊔ Australia

33. In which European city was the ballet producer and director Dame Marie Rambert born?
- ⊔ Warsaw
- ⊔ Madrid
- ⊔ Berlin

34. What term describes a newly elected Parliament in which no party has an overall majority?
- ⊔ Hung Parliament
- ⊔ Crossed Parliament
- ⊔ Spillover Parliament

35. In 2005, Gordon Brown became the MP for which constituency?
- ⊔ Lanark and Hamilton East
- ⊔ Kirkcaldy and Cowdenbeath
- ⊔ Ochil and South Perthshire

36. What is the meaning of the word 'fecund'?
- ⊔ Bursting
- ⊔ Fertile
- ⊔ Shiny

ANSWERS ON P.272

37. What is the official language of the Central American country Guatemala?
  - ⊔ French
  - ⊔ Spanish
  - ⊔ Portuguese

38. Which actress won an Oscar for her performance in the 1940 film *Kitty Foyle*?
  - ⊔ Rita Hayworth
  - ⊔ Joan Fontaine
  - ⊔ Ginger Rogers

39. Which word is used to describe pottery that is made up of different coloured scraps of clay?
  - ⊔ Scroddled
  - ⊔ Groodled
  - ⊔ Trinkled

40. 'The Lilywhites' is the nickname of which regiment of the British Army?
  - ⊔ The Scots Guards
  - ⊔ The Coldstream Guards
  - ⊔ The Parachute Regiment

41. What term is used to describe an allowance for daily expenses, such as that given to actors on location?
  - ⊔ Ad Hoc
  - ⊔ Sub Rosa
  - ⊔ Per Diem

42. 'Dogfight' is a term especially used to describe combat between what?
  - ⊔ Tanks
  - ⊔ Fighter Planes
  - ⊔ Submarines

ANSWERS ON P.272

43. In October 2007, it was announced that which country will host the 2014 FIFA World Cup?
- South Africa
- Brazil
- China

44. Caisson Disease is another name for which condition?
- Amnesia
- The Bends
- Bleeding Gums

45. Sir Edwin Lutyens is particularly associated with the urban planning of which Indian city?
- Mumbai
- Chandigarh
- New Delhi

46. Which of the Queen's grandchildren was born on the 21st of June 1982?
- Zara Phillips
- Princess Beatrice
- Prince William

47. In Roman times, what was the profession of a 'publican'?
- Textile Dealer
- Arrow Maker
- Tax Collector

48. The line 'Into each life some rain must fall' comes from a poem called *The Rainy Day* by which poet?
- Dryden
- Longfellow
- Tennyson

ANSWERS ON P.272

49. **What type of creature is the Avahi Cleesei – named after the actor John Cleese?**

- Wombat
- Kangaroo
- Lemur

50. **What name is given to the era that started in Japan in January 1989?**

- Heisei
- Taisho
- Showa

51. **Benjamin Disraeli was Prime Minister during the reign of which British monarch?**

- William IV
- Queen Victoria
- Edward VII

52. **Which man, born in 1815, was the first person to serve as the Chancellor of Germany?**

- Blucher
- Bismarck
- Hindenburg

53. **According to *The Concise Oxford English Dictionary*, when used in a text message, for what do the letters BTW stand?**

- By The Way
- Before The Weekend
- Between These Walls

54. **The Lamaze Technique is the name of a method used in which process?**

- Childbirth
- Acting
- Fortune Telling

ANSWERS ON P.272

55. In the game of chess, which piece stands between the Castle and Bishop at the start of the game?
    ⊔ King
    ⊔ Queen
    ⊔ Knight

56. 'Beak' is an old-fashioned slang term for which profession?
    ⊔ Magistrate
    ⊔ Policeman
    ⊔ Barber

57. Which opera by Verdi is based on Victor Hugo's play *Le roi s'amuse*?
    ⊔ La Traviata
    ⊔ Nabucco
    ⊔ Rigoletto

58. Which country was the first in the world to have a complete system of plastic, or polymer, bank notes?
    ⊔ Australia
    ⊔ United States
    ⊔ United Kingdom

59. Badgers live in communities within an extensive network of burrows known as a what?
    ⊔ Sett
    ⊔ Drey
    ⊔ Holt

60. Peggy Guggenheim is a name associated with which field of the arts?
    ⊔ Ballet
    ⊔ Opera
    ⊔ Visual Art

ANSWERS ON P.272

61. Lithium, sodium, potassium, rubidium and francium are elements belonging to which group in the Periodic Table?
- ␣ Noble Gases
- ␣ Alkali Metals
- ␣ Lanthanides

62. Which writer, born in Dublin in 1856, won the 1925 Nobel Prize for Literature?
- ␣ James Joyce
- ␣ Samuel Beckett
- ␣ George Bernard Shaw

63. In which role is Patrick Demarchelier famous in the field of fashion?
- ␣ Designer
- ␣ Model
- ␣ Photographer

64. What is the official name for a male duck?
- ␣ Cob
- ␣ Drake
- ␣ Pen

65. Which alcoholic spirit is an essential ingredient of a Cuba Libre?
- ␣ Rum
- ␣ Whisky
- ␣ Gin

66. What is the profession of Frasier Crane in the US sitcom *Frasier*?
- ␣ Architect
- ␣ Psychiatrist
- ␣ Gardener

ANSWERS ON P.272

67. What year formed the title of a UK hit single for James Blunt in 2007?
- ⊔ 1963
- ⊔ 1973
- ⊔ 1983

68. Where was the chef Ken Hom born?
- ⊔ Tucson, Arizona
- ⊔ Milan, Italy
- ⊔ Nice, France

69. The gold coin called the Krugerrand is minted in which country?
- ⊔ South Africa
- ⊔ Germany
- ⊔ New Zealand

70. Which car manufacturer produces the Golf and Fox models?
- ⊔ Volkswagen
- ⊔ Ford
- ⊔ Vauxhall

71. The 'tabs' is another word for which part of a theatre?
- ⊔ The Wings
- ⊔ The Stage Curtains
- ⊔ The Dressing Rooms

72. What was the real surname of the author Nevil Shute?
- ⊔ Denmark
- ⊔ Sweden
- ⊔ Norway

ANSWERS ON P.272

73. Which celebrated actress has, for many years, been an outspoken animal rights activist?
⌐ Jeanne Moreau
⌐ Brigitte Bardot
⌐ Leslie Caron

74. What type of bridge is the Forth Railway Bridge over the Firth of Forth in Scotland?
⌐ Truss
⌐ Bascule
⌐ Cantilever

75. Lucy Honeychurch is the central character of which novel?
⌐ A Room With a View
⌐ Robinson Crusoe
⌐ Wuthering Heights

76. 001 is the international dialling code for which country?
⌐ Germany
⌐ USA
⌐ France

77. Which philosopher wrote *Our Knowledge of the External World* and was awarded the Nobel Prize for Literature in 1950?
⌐ Immanuel Kant
⌐ Bertrand Russell
⌐ Friedrich Nietzsche

78. In India, what is a 'punkah'?
⌐ A Fan
⌐ A Refrigerator
⌐ A Pantry

ANSWERS ON P.272

79. Which member of the Royal Family married for the first time in 1973?
- ⌣ Princess Margaret
- ⌣ Princess Anne
- ⌣ Prince Charles

80. The British company Boosey & Hawkes are well known as what type of publishers?
- ⌣ Romance Novels
- ⌣ Maps
- ⌣ Music

81. What is the disposition of a person described as 'saturnine'?
- ⌣ Delicate
- ⌣ Drunk
- ⌣ Gloomy

82. Cachalot is another term for which creature?
- ⌣ Sperm Whale
- ⌣ Tawny Owl
- ⌣ Honey Bee

83. The song 'Tea For Two' was originally introduced in which musical?
- ⌣ 42nd Street
- ⌣ No, No, Nanette
- ⌣ Charlie Girl

84. The Akita is a breed of which animal?
- ⌣ Horse
- ⌣ Rabbit
- ⌣ Dog

ANSWERS ON P.272

85. How frequently does something described as 'quotidian' take place?
- ⌴ Hourly
- ⌴ Daily
- ⌴ Yearly

86. In which year did the Chinese Army infamously open fire on a group of protesters in Beijing's Tiananmen Square?
- ⌴ 1969
- ⌴ 1979
- ⌴ 1989

87. What type of plant is featured on the Northern Irish version of a one pound coin first issued in 1986?
- ⌴ A Flax Plant
- ⌴ A Daffodil
- ⌴ A Bluebell

88. What is the literal meaning of the Japanese word 'ninja'?
- ⌴ Teacher
- ⌴ Protector
- ⌴ Spy

89. What was traditionally contained in a 'pouncet box'?
- ⌴ Slippers
- ⌴ Perfume
- ⌴ Matches

90. Which British actor provided the voice for the title character in the 2007 film *Beowulf*?
- ⌴ Patrick Stewart
- ⌴ Ray Winstone
- ⌴ Jude Law

ANSWERS ON P.272

91. The expression 'squeaky clean' is derived from which activity?
- ␛ Pig Breeding
- ␛ Hair Washing
- ␛ Roller-Skating

92. What is the most common surname in Germany?
- ␛ Weiss
- ␛ Müller
- ␛ Schneider

93. Which British racing driver won the British Formula 1 Grand Prix a total of five times?
- ␛ Jim Clark
- ␛ Nigel Mansell
- ␛ Damon Hill

94. The city of Stoke-on-Trent is famous for the production of what material?
- ␛ Lace
- ␛ Pottery
- ␛ Silk

95. The term 'Mardi Gras' is derived from an old French phrase meaning what?
- ␛ Fat Tuesday
- ␛ Big Wednesday
- ␛ Black Thursday

96. What type of creature is a daphnia?
- ␛ Wood Louse
- ␛ Water Flea
- ␛ Sea Slug

ANSWERS ON P.272

97. 'Domenica' is the Italian word for which day of the week?
⊔ Sunday
⊔ Tuesday
⊔ Thursday

98. 'Yellowbelly' is a term given to people born and bred in which part of the United Kingdom?
⊔ Lincolnshire
⊔ Powys
⊔ Forfarshire

99. 'Here comes a chopper to chop off your head' is a line from which nursery rhyme?
⊔ Oranges and Lemons
⊔ Ding Dong Bell
⊔ Goosey, Goosey Gander

100. In which field of the arts was Wilhelm Furtwängler a leading name in the 20th century?
⊔ Fashion
⊔ Conducting
⊔ Ballet

ANSWERS ON P.272

KEVIN ASHMAN

FULL NAME:
Kevin Clifford Ashman

HOME TOWN:
Winchester

EDUCATION:
St Bede's Primary School, Peter Symonds Grammar School/College, Southampton University. 8 O-levels, 3 A-levels, 1 S-level and BA (in modern history).

QUIZZING CREDENTIALS:
Off-screen: 4 world championships, 6 European championships, 9 British championships, 11 Brain of London titles and 10 Magnum Trophies (Mastermind Club individual).
Onscreen: *Mastermind* 1995, *Brain of Britain* 1996 (followed by various offshoots of these such as *Brain of Brains* and *Top Brain*, both 1998), and *Masterbrain* (a hybrid of the two shows) 1995 and 1996.
Fifteen to One champion 1989 and 1999 (Millennium special).

LEAST FAVOURITE EGGHEADS SUBJECT:
Food and Drink.

SPECIAL INTEREST/HOBBIES (AMALGAMATED BECAUSE I DON'T UNDERSTAND THE DIFFERENCE):
History (and current affairs), cinema, theatre, the arts generally, travel, sport (watching!), and lots of general reading.

WHAT DOES IT TAKE TO BE AN EGGHEAD:
Obviously a very retentive memory and a wide-ranging general knowledge, but crucially also speed of recall – there's usually a time element in quizzing. Another point is that practice makes perfect (or that's the theory). Take part in as many quizzes as you can, and if possible join a league. Admittedly that's easier in some places than others, but they're worth searching out. The regular competition at a good level (and with like-minded people who are also into quizzing) really does boost experience and confidence.

WHO WOULD BE ON YOUR ULTIMATE FANTASY QUIZ TEAM:
My first thought would be geniuses/polymaths such as Einstein, Shakespeare, etc. But would they necessarily be good quizzers? A certain Monty Python sketch springs to mind. Any quiz team hoping for success needs a good blend of people whose expertise covers as wide a spectrum of potential subjects as possible. So whether we're talking about fantasy figures or real-life top quiz players, it all becomes 'how long is a piece of string' speculation. As a quick answer, and sticking with pure fantasy, I think the best bet for victory would be the likes of Stalin or Genghis Khan. After all, who's going to argue or contradict them (apart from Daphne)?

MOST MEMORABLE MOMENT AS EGGHEAD:
It's all been memorable, but I suppose reaching a major milestone such as the 1000th show has to rank highly; not many shows achieve that.

ADVICE FOR BUDDING EGGHEADS:
Read and watch! There's no real substitute for the wide-ranging approach mentioned above. It's always a good idea to keep up with current events, because there'll always be a proportion of questions based on recent stuff.

FAVOURITE FACT OR PIECE OF TRIVIA:
For me, there's no such thing. It's all worth knowing, and my heart sinks when, as has happened many times over the years, someone asks me 'What's your favourite quiz question?' Once I've been asked a question – successfully or unsuccessfully – I pass on to the next one; I don't even remember the questions that clinched titles for me, which might otherwise be considered contenders as favourites. So it'll all have to remain one of life's little mysteries.

LITTLE KNOWN FACT:
I was Daniel Craig's stunt double for the Bond films. No, I lied there. We'll stick to quizzing. Before *Eggheads*, my highest profile was probably achieved when I won *Mastermind* in 1995 and (in the first round) got the still record score on the show of 41. But I wasn't even one of the original line-up of contestants that year, I was a reserve, and only took part because somebody had to drop out. You never know what's around the corner!

1. The soldier known as El Cid is a famous character in the history of which country?
   - ⸆ Brazil
   - ⸆ Spain
   - ⸆ Scotland

2. The Roman invasion of Britain took place in which year?
   - ⸆ 43 AD
   - ⸆ 143 AD
   - ⸆ 243 AD

3. Which aviation pioneer, born in 1898, disappeared over the Pacific Ocean during a round-the-world flight in 1937?
   - ⸆ Louis Bleriot
   - ⸆ Joseph Montgolfier
   - ⸆ Amelia Earhart

4. What job did Wyatt Earp famously perform in the American Wild West?
   - ⸆ Lawman
   - ⸆ Army Scout
   - ⸆ Rancher

5. The Battle of Kursk of July 1943 was fought between the armoured divisions of the German army and which other country?
   - ⸆ United States
   - ⸆ Soviet Union
   - ⸆ France

6. The Dambusters Raid of 1943 primarily targeted dams in which German valley?
   - ⸆ The Ruhr Valley
   - ⸆ The Rhine Valley
   - ⸆ The Elbe Valley

ANSWERS ON P.273

7. 'Pride's Purge' is the name given to an incident during the reign of which English monarch?
- ⊔ Charles I
- ⊔ Richard III
- ⊔ Elizabeth I

8. The American Civil War was fought between the North and an alliance of states known by what name?
- ⊔ Coalition
- ⊔ Communion
- ⊔ Confederacy

9. The name of which historical people is thought to translate as 'one who lurks in a bay' or 'pirate'?
- ⊔ Normans
- ⊔ Goths
- ⊔ Vikings

10. Who did Percy Shelley describe as 'an old, mad, blind, despised and dying king'?
- ⊔ George III
- ⊔ William IV
- ⊔ Edward VII

11. 'Adlertag' or 'Eagle Day' in 1940 signalled the start of what?
- ⊔ The Phoney War
- ⊔ The German Invasion of Russia
- ⊔ The Battle of Britain

12. The Modern Olympic Games derive from an athletic festival of which ancient civilisation?
- ⊔ Greek
- ⊔ Roman
- ⊔ Carthaginian

ANSWERS ON P.273

13. What name was given to the individual secret illegal
    drinking dens that opened up during prohibition in the USA?
    ⊔ Speakslowlies
    ⊔ Speaksmoothlies
    ⊔ Speakeasies

14. 'The Night of the Long Knives' was the name given to a
    series of political executions in which country in 1934?
    ⊔ Soviet Union
    ⊔ Germany
    ⊔ China

15. What type of Roman gladiator was known as the 'fish man'
    or 'fish fighter'?
    ⊔ Hoplomachus
    ⊔ Murmillo
    ⊔ Galerus

16. Which Anglo-Saxon king was baptised by St Augustine in
    597 AD?
    ⊔ Ethelbert
    ⊔ Hengist
    ⊔ Offa

17. In which county was the locomotive pioneer Richard
    Trevithick born?
    ⊔ Norfolk
    ⊔ Cornwall
    ⊔ Cumbria

18. The English army's mastery of which weapon has been
    credited with their success at the Battle of Crécy during the
    Hundred Years' War?
    ⊔ The Musket
    ⊔ The Catapult
    ⊔ The Longbow

ANSWERS ON P.273

19. The Mausoleum of Maussollos, one of the seven ancient wonders of the world, was built in which modern day country?
    ⊔ Turkey
    ⊔ Iraq
    ⊔ Tunisia

20. Which American general of World War II was famous for using a corn-cob pipe?
    ⊔ Eisenhower
    ⊔ MacArthur
    ⊔ Patton

21. Which journalist and media figure famously spoke out against Joseph McCarthy on his *See It Now* programme in 1954?
    ⊔ Edward Murrow
    ⊔ Walter Kronkite
    ⊔ Dan Rather

22. Which company owned the cruise liner *Lusitania* which was controversially sunk by German torpedoes in 1915?
    ⊔ Ellerman Lines
    ⊔ White Star Line
    ⊔ Cunard

23. In which century was the census known as the Domesday Book compiled?
    ⊔ 9th
    ⊔ 11th
    ⊔ 13th

24. Which emperor, born in 76 AD, is famous for halting the expansion of the Roman Empire and building fortifications along the boundaries of its territory?
    ⊔ Caligula
    ⊔ Diocletian
    ⊔ Hadrian

ANSWERS ON P.273

25. In which year was the Indian politician Rajiv Gandhi assassinated?
    - ⊔ 1981
    - ⊔ 1991
    - ⊔ 2001

26. In 1960, Israeli agents tracked down the Nazi war criminal Adolf Eichmann in which country?
    - ⊔ Argentina
    - ⊔ Algeria
    - ⊔ Austria

27. When he died in 1916, Franz-Joseph, the long-serving Emperor of Austria, had been on the throne for how many years?
    - ⊔ 48
    - ⊔ 58
    - ⊔ 68

28. In 1864, in one of the biggest man-made disasters in British history, the bursting of the Dale Dyke Dam flooded which city?
    - ⊔ Peterborough
    - ⊔ Birmingham
    - ⊔ Sheffield

29. The period of British history known as the Industrial Revolution is commonly said to have begun in which century?
    - ⊔ 14th
    - ⊔ 16th
    - ⊔ 18th

30. By what name was William Cody of the American Wild West better known?
    - ⊔ Wild Bill Hickok
    - ⊔ Buffalo Bill
    - ⊔ Billy the Kid

ANSWERS ON P.273

31. The ill-fated Princes in the Tower, believed to have been murdered in 1483, were the sons of which king?
⊔ Edward IV
⊔ Henry III
⊔ Richard II

32. In ancient Rome, senators wore togas trimmed with a broad stripe of which colour as a sign of their status?
⊔ Black
⊔ Purple
⊔ Green

33. Eric Bloodaxe was a king of which people in the 10th century AD?
⊔ The Moors
⊔ The Celts
⊔ The Vikings

34. What name was given to the tight, porcupine-like formation typically used by the Hoplite armies of the ancient Greeks?
⊔ The Wedge
⊔ The Testudo
⊔ The Phalanx

35. In which year did the British East India Company establish its first trading post on the Indian subcontinent at Surat?
⊔ 1412
⊔ 1612
⊔ 1812

36. The treaty known as the Peace of Vereeniging marked the end of which period of history?
⊔ The Boer Wars
⊔ The 100 Years' War
⊔ The French Revolution

ANSWERS ON P.273

37. What is the literal meaning of Mohandas K. Gandhi's honorary title 'Mahatma'?
- ⊔ Great Warrior
- ⊔ Great Soul
- ⊔ Great Father

38. Which company manufactured the Hurricane – one of the planes accountable for the RAF's success in the Battle of Britain?
- ⊔ Westland
- ⊔ Hawker
- ⊔ Vickers-Armstrongs

39. The October Crisis of 1970, in which the politicians James Cross and Pierre Laporte were kidnapped, took place in which country?
- ⊔ Switzerland
- ⊔ France
- ⊔ Canada

40. Which country gained independence from the British Crown in 1964 with Kenneth Kaunda becoming President?
- ⊔ Zambia
- ⊔ Kenya
- ⊔ Zimbabwe

41. What was the name of the California hotel in which Senator Robert Kennedy was shot in 1968?
- ⊔ Chateau Marmont Hotel
- ⊔ Hotel Bel-Air
- ⊔ Ambassador Hotel

42. What was the name of the colony established by the Mayflower pilgrims in 1620 in what is now Massachusetts?
- ⊔ Southampton
- ⊔ Portsmouth
- ⊔ Plymouth

ANSWERS ON P.273

43. Which Mediterranean island became a British Crown Colony by the 1814 Treaty of Paris?
⊔ Crete
⊔ Malta
⊔ Corsica

44. What was the name of the Norman King of Sicily from 1130 to 1154?
⊔ Stephen I
⊔ Roger II
⊔ Leo III

45. During World War II, what was the official combatant status of Eire, now the Republic of Ireland?
⊔ Pro-Allies
⊔ Neutral
⊔ Pro-Axis

46. 'Prince Rupert' was a military commander in which conflict?
⊔ Wars of the Roses
⊔ English Civil War
⊔ Napoleonic Wars

47. What was the name of the French diplomat responsible for the construction of the Suez Canal?
⊔ Guy de Maupassant
⊔ Simon de Montfort
⊔ Ferdinand de Lesseps

48. A piece of armour known as a 'gorget' was worn to protect which part of the body?
⊔ Throat
⊔ Ankle
⊔ Shoulder

ANSWERS ON P.273

49. The threshing machine, invented by Andrew Meikle in the 18th century, was used in which industry?
   ⊔ Agriculture
   ⊔ Textiles
   ⊔ Mining

50. What name was given to labourers employed in the excavation and construction of roads, railways or canals?
   ⊔ Hillbillies
   ⊔ Navvies
   ⊔ Clippies

51. Which of Henry VIII's wives is buried next to him in St George's Chapel at Windsor Castle?
   ⊔ Anne Boleyn
   ⊔ Catherine of Aragon
   ⊔ Jane Seymour

52. What was the first name of Lord Kitchener, Secretary of State for War in the first years of World War I?
   ⊔ Henry
   ⊔ Harold
   ⊔ Horatio

53. What name was given to the open courtyard area of medieval castles?
   ⊔ Motte
   ⊔ Bailey
   ⊔ Keep

54. Which subject did the Latin American revolutionary Ernesto 'Che' Guevara study at university?
   ⊔ Medicine
   ⊔ Law
   ⊔ Architecture

ANSWERS ON P.273

55. The celebrated traveller Marco Polo was born and died in which Italian city?
- ⊔ Milan
- ⊔ Venice
- ⊔ Genoa

56. Jehosaphat was king of which ancient region in the 9th century BC?
- ⊔ Hibernia
- ⊔ Judah
- ⊔ Mauritania

57. What type of transport is a Blimp, used during World War I?
- ⊔ Airship
- ⊔ Tank
- ⊔ Submarine

58. The Scotsman John McAdam, born in 1756, was a famous name in which field?
- ⊔ Canals
- ⊔ Aviation
- ⊔ Road Building

59. 'La Pucelle' is a nickname of which historical figure?
- ⊔ Joan of Arc
- ⊔ Napoleon
- ⊔ Charles de Gaulle

60. The infamous Doctor Crippen was arrested on board which ship in 1910?
- ⊔ HMS Forfar
- ⊔ RMS Queen Mary
- ⊔ SS Montrose

ANSWERS ON P.273

61. The Siege of Lucknow occurred during which conflict?
- ⊔ Indian Mutiny
- ⊔ Crimean War
- ⊔ American Revolution

62. Who, in the 19th century, invented the phonograph?
- ⊔ Thomas Edison
- ⊔ Benjamin Franklin
- ⊔ Alexander Graham Bell

63. Danelaw was the area of Anglo-Saxon England between the Thames and which other river?
- ⊔ River Tees
- ⊔ River Severn
- ⊔ River Nene

64. In the 6th to the 8th centuries AD, 'Austrasia' was a kingdom in which continent?
- ⊔ Europe
- ⊔ South America
- ⊔ Africa

65. Who was the third and final husband of the Italian noblewoman Lucrezia Borgia?
- ⊔ Giovanni Sforza
- ⊔ Alfonso d'Este
- ⊔ Virginio Orsini

66. Aga was the title given to an official in which empire?
- ⊔ Aztec
- ⊔ Ottoman
- ⊔ Roman

67. What nickname did the Duke of Wellington's men give him?
- ⊔ Nosey
- ⊔ Boney
- ⊔ Skinny

68. What type of weapon was the 'Tiger', produced by Germany during World War II?
- ⊔ Jet Fighter
- ⊔ Tank
- ⊔ Submarine

69. The Sabines were an ancient tribe of which country?
- ⊔ Netherlands
- ⊔ Egypt
- ⊔ Italy

70. Burghley and Walsingham were trusted advisors to which English monarch?
- ⊔ Richard III
- ⊔ Elizabeth I
- ⊔ Victoria

71. Nimrud and Khorsabad were capitals of which ancient empire?
- ⊔ Assyrian
- ⊔ Greek
- ⊔ Inca

72. According to diarist John Evelyn, the stones of which building 'flew like grenades' during the Great Fire of London?
- ⊔ Lambeth Palace
- ⊔ St Paul's Cathedral
- ⊔ Tower of London

ANSWERS ON P.273

73. The Valley of the Kings contains the burial places of which rulers?
⊔ Pharaohs
⊔ Caesars
⊔ Sheikhs

74. Which stadium of ancient Rome was built to stage gladiatorial contests?
⊔ The Circus Maximus
⊔ The Colosseum
⊔ The Pantheon

75. Which explorer died in the Philippines in 1521 while attempting to circumnavigate the globe?
⊔ Marco Polo
⊔ Christopher Columbus
⊔ Ferdinand Magellan

76. The NKVD was the secret police agency of which country?
⊔ France
⊔ Soviet Union
⊔ Italy

77. Which member of Rome's First Triumvirate was defeated by the Parthians at the Battle of Carrhae in 53 BC?
⊔ Crassus
⊔ Caesar
⊔ Pompey

78. In which century in Britain did the so-called 'Hungry Forties' take place?
⊔ 19th
⊔ 18th
⊔ 17th

ANSWERS ON P.273

79. The 'Pilgrim Fathers' who colonised North America in the 17th century were followers of which form of Christianity?
   ⌐ Unification Church
   ⌐ Mormonism
   ⌐ Puritanism

80. What was the name of Admiral Nelson's flagship at the Battle of Trafalgar?
   ⌐ HMS Victory
   ⌐ The Golden Hinde
   ⌐ HMS Vanguard

81. An experimental camp on Brownsea Island in Poole Harbour in 1907 led directly to the establishment of which organisation?
   ⌐ SAS
   ⌐ RSPB
   ⌐ Boy Scouts

82. What title was held by minor parish officials in Britain whose role included ushering and preserving order?
   ⌐ Mercer
   ⌐ Beadle
   ⌐ Fletcher

83. In September 1943, 191 British servicemen downed their weapons and refused to fight in which battle of World War II?
   ⌐ The Battle of the Bulge
   ⌐ The Battle of Arnhem
   ⌐ The Battle of Salerno

84. Which series of fortifications built by the Romans in Scotland predates Hadrian's Wall by around fifty years?
   The Greg Line
   The Gask Ridge
   The Dunkeld Dyke

ANSWERS ON P.273

85. Commonly used by European knights in the medieval period, what was 'chainmail'?
- ⊔ Weapon
- ⊔ Body Armour
- ⊔ Shield

86. A person involved in which historical occupation would be heard to shout 'Stand and deliver'?
- ⊔ Hangman
- ⊔ Highwayman
- ⊔ Chimney Sweep

87. What nickname was given to the standard British infantry musket in the 18th century?
- ⊔ Green Gertie
- ⊔ Brown Bess
- ⊔ Black Bronwen

88. Which grief-stricken Roman emperor made his consort into a god after he drowned in the Nile in 130 AD?
- ⊔ Antoninus Pius
- ⊔ Trajan
- ⊔ Hadrian

89. What name is given to chopped up pieces of precious metal used as currency by the Vikings?
- ⊔ Hacksilver
- ⊔ Sheargold
- ⊔ Slicebronze

90. The 1861 Emancipation of the Serfs marked the beginning of the end of feudalism in which country?
- ⊔ Russia
- ⊔ France
- ⊔ Japan

ANSWERS ON P.273

91. The ancient kingdom of Sheba was located in which part of the world?
    ⌣ Central Asia
    ⌣ The Arabian Peninsula
    ⌣ Southern Africa

92. Which US President was the first to address the American people on television?
    ⌣ Theodore Roosevelt
    ⌣ Franklin D. Roosevelt
    ⌣ Dwight D. Eisenhower

93. Which of Europe's dictators did Violet Gibson attempt to assassinate in 1926?
    ⌣ Hitler
    ⌣ Stalin
    ⌣ Mussolini

94. Which creatures, later to become England's national emblem, did Richard I use on his personal coat of arms?
    ⌣ Stags
    ⌣ Lions
    ⌣ Cocks

95. What general name is given to the poverty relief laws of the Tudor period and the subsequent 1834 amendment?
    ⌣ Poor Laws
    ⌣ Beggar Laws
    ⌣ Vagrancy Laws

96. Which ancient record features the Latin words 'Hic Harold Rex Interfectus Est'?
    ⌣ Magna Carta
    ⌣ Bayeux Tapestry
    ⌣ Mappa Mundi

ANSWERS ON P.273

97. Which social class was regarded as the most prestigious in ancient Rome?
⊔ Senatorial
⊔ Equestrian
⊔ Plebeian

98. Which French monarch was nicknamed 'the Well-Beloved'?
⊔ Louis XIV
⊔ Louis XV
⊔ Louis XVI

99. The 'boneshaker' was an early type of which form of transport?
⊔ Hot Air Balloon
⊔ Helicopter
⊔ Bicycle

100. Which British Home Secretary caused controversy for his part in the Derek Bentley case of 1953?
⊔ Rab Butler
⊔ James Callaghan
⊔ David Maxwell Fyfe

ANSWERS ON P.273

GENERAL KNOWLEDGE

1. Who purchased Virgin Radio from Richard Branson in 1997?
   - ⊔ Chris Evans
   - ⊔ Jonathan Ross
   - ⊔ Johnny Vaughan

2. The term 'pundit', used to mean an expert in a certain field, is derived from which language?
   - ⊔ Greek
   - ⊔ Inuit
   - ⊔ Sanskrit

3. The cricketer W.G. Grace was born near which city?
   - ⊔ Norwich
   - ⊔ Bristol
   - ⊔ York

4. Inhabitants of which Scottish town call themselves 'Buddies'?
   - ⊔ Cromarty
   - ⊔ Paisley
   - ⊔ Troon

5. Which tennis player is nicknamed the 'Beast of Belarus'?
   - ⊔ Novak Djokovic
   - ⊔ Max Mirnyi
   - ⊔ Ivo Karlovic

6. 'You're gonna need a bigger boat' is a famous quote from which Steven Spielberg film?
   - ⊔ Hook
   - ⊔ Jurassic Park
   - ⊔ Jaws

ANSWERS ON P.274

7. What type of sword are you said to 'rattle' if you make a display or threat of military force?
   - ⌴ Sabre
   - ⌴ Foil
   - ⌴ Broadsword

8. What name is given to an extravagant, costly and generally non-functional building?
   - ⌴ Vagary
   - ⌴ Folly
   - ⌴ Whim

9. *The Lexicon of Love* was a UK number one album in 1982 for which group?
   - ⌴ Spandau Ballet
   - ⌴ ABC
   - ⌴ Haircut 100

10. 'Jiggers' and 'jolleys' were machines once widely used in British factories to make what?
    - ⌴ Ceramics
    - ⌴ Steel
    - ⌴ Books

11. According to Greek mythology, what did Cadmus sow in the ground?
    - ⌴ Dragon's Teeth
    - ⌴ Minotaur's Blood
    - ⌴ Aphrodite's Hair

12. What is the full first name of the former US Vice-President Al Gore?
    - ⌴ Albert
    - ⌴ Alan
    - ⌴ Alexander

ANSWERS ON P.274

13. Christine and Raoul are the central characters of which Andrew Lloyd Webber musical?
  - ⌐ Sunset Boulevard
  - ⌐ The Phantom of the Opera
  - ⌐ The Woman in White

14. According to Cole Porter's song, who 'regrets. She's unable to lunch today'?
  - ⌐ Miss Daisy
  - ⌐ Miss Otis
  - ⌐ Miss Saigon

15. Which philosopher is believed to have come up with many of his theories whilst sitting in an oven?
  - ⌐ Descartes
  - ⌐ Voltaire
  - ⌐ Machiavelli

16. Which shrub is also known as the 'butterfly bush'?
  - ⌐ Buddleia
  - ⌐ Bougainvillea
  - ⌐ Forsythia

17. Which informal expression is used to describe rigid bureaucratic rules?
  - ⌐ Red Book
  - ⌐ Red Tape
  - ⌐ Red Brick

18. *High Noon*, made in 1952, is an example of what type of film?
  - ⌐ Western
  - ⌐ Musical
  - ⌐ Gangster

ANSWERS ON P.274

19. Which North American grazing animal takes its name from an Algonquin word meaning 'eater of twigs'?
    ⊔ Buffalo
    ⊔ Moose
    ⊔ Sheep

20. 'Let slip the dogs of war' and 'the evil that men do' are lines from which Shakespeare play?
    ⊔ Twelfth Night
    ⊔ Hamlet
    ⊔ Julius Caesar

21. In which region of the Asian subcontinent did the form of music and dance called bhangra originate?
    ⊔ Assam
    ⊔ Punjab
    ⊔ Tamil Nadu

22. In which year was George W. Bush first inaugurated as the President of the USA?
    ⊔ 1997
    ⊔ 1999
    ⊔ 2001

23. In the UK, which term is used to refer to a parliamentary year?
    ⊔ Journal
    ⊔ Division
    ⊔ Session

24. Purim is a holiday celebrated in which religion?
    ⊔ Islam
    ⊔ Hinduism
    ⊔ Judaism

ANSWERS ON P.274

25. The Italian product bresaola is made from which type of meat?

⊔ Beef

⊔ Pork

⊔ Lamb

26. In which decade did the transport aircraft known as the Spruce Goose make its maiden and only flight?

⊔ 1920s

⊔ 1930s

⊔ 1940s

27. DJ Norman Cook was formally a bassist for which band?

⊔ The Bluebells

⊔ The Housemartins

⊔ The Levellers

28. What is the name of the species of spider which captures its prey by swinging a 'lasso' of sticky silk?

⊔ Bolas Spider

⊔ Huntsman Spider

⊔ Recluse Spider

29. Appledore and Sage Derby are types of what?

⊔ Cheese

⊔ Nut

⊔ Fish

30. Which Italian city is served by Cristoforo Colombo international airport?

⊔ Rome

⊔ Genoa

⊔ Naples

ANSWERS ON P.274

31. The Snowy Mountains are part of which mountain range?
- ⊔ Southern Alps
- ⊔ Australian Alps
- ⊔ Appalachians

32. In August 1934, after a spell in the Atlanta penitentiary, Al Capone was transferred to which prison?
- ⊔ San Quentin
- ⊔ Sing Sing
- ⊔ Alcatraz

33. What name is given to a French sauce made with Madeira and truffles?
- ⊔ Financière
- ⊔ Florentine
- ⊔ Flauntière

34. 'P' is the international vehicle registration letter of which country?
- ⊔ Poland
- ⊔ Portugal
- ⊔ Peru

35. Of which organisation was Janet Street-Porter the president in the 1990s?
- ⊔ Ramblers' Association
- ⊔ RSPCA
- ⊔ Red Cross

36. The United States Naval Academy is situated in which city?
- ⊔ Minneapolis
- ⊔ Annapolis
- ⊔ Indianapolis

ANSWERS ON P.274

37. What are the syndicates of private underwriters at Lloyd's of London known as?
⊔ Marks
⊔ Names
⊔ Sahibs

38. Which ancient Greek playwright wrote *The Bacchae*?
⊔ Aristophanes
⊔ Euripides
⊔ Sophocles

39. What is the first name of the wife of the former British Prime Minister John Major?
⊔ Norma
⊔ Ursula
⊔ Sarah

40. Which part of the human body is affected by tartar?
⊔ Hair
⊔ Nails
⊔ Teeth

41. In February 2008, it was announced that which children's TV programme was to be axed after thirty years?
⊔ Jackanory
⊔ Grange Hill
⊔ Blue Peter

42. Which constituent part of the flag known as the Union Jack consists of 'saltire argent in a field azure'?
⊔ Cross of St Andrew
⊔ Cross of St George
⊔ Cross of St Patrick

ANSWERS ON P.274

43. Who became the first senior royal to receive an award in the 2007 New Years Honours List?
- ⌴ Prince William
- ⌴ Sophie Wessex
- ⌴ Zara Phillips

44. Hermann's, marginated and Horsfield's are types of which creature?
- ⌴ Chinchilla
- ⌴ Tortoise
- ⌴ Donkey

45. Which *X Factor* singer reached the top of the UK singles chart in April 2010 with 'Once'?
- ⌴ Lucie Jones
- ⌴ Stacey Solomon
- ⌴ Diana Vickers

46. In the final film of Sergio Leone's 'Man with No Name' trilogy, Clint Eastwood plays which of the three title characters?
- ⌴ The Good
- ⌴ The Bad
- ⌴ The Ugly

47. The towns of Ayr and Troon are located on which body of water?
- ⌴ Moray Firth
- ⌴ Firth of Forth
- ⌴ Firth of Clyde

48. In January 2008, James Castrission and Justin Jones crossed the Tasman Sea from Australia to New Zealand in what type of vessel?
- ⌴ Sloop
- ⌴ Jetski
- ⌴ Kayak

ANSWERS ON P.274

49. Alaa-Al-Aswanys's best-selling novel *The Yacoubian Building* is set in which city?
- ⌣ Cairo
- ⌣ Rabat
- ⌣ Tripoli

50. Which musical instrument is called 'das Fagott' in German and 'il fagotto' in Italian?
- ⌣ Violin
- ⌣ Bassoon
- ⌣ Trombone

51. What term is used for a large gathering of Scouts or Guides?
- ⌣ Shindig
- ⌣ Jamboree
- ⌣ Junket

52. Which superhero is famously vulnerable to kryptonite?
- ⌣ Batman
- ⌣ Spider-Man
- ⌣ Superman

53. What code name was used for the top secret British nuclear weapon programme during World War II?
- ⌣ Iron Pipes
- ⌣ Tube Alloys
- ⌣ Steel Bars

54. The ancient road known as the Salarian Way led from Rome to which Adriatic port?
- ⌣ Ancona
- ⌣ Pescara
- ⌣ Bari

ANSWERS ON P.274

55. Bernard Haitink is a famous name in which field?
  ⌐⌐ Conducting
  ⌐⌐ Painting
  ⌐⌐ Writing

56. What does the nautical term 'weigh anchor' mean?
  ⌐⌐ Raise the Anchor
  ⌐⌐ Lower the Anchor
  ⌐⌐ Polish the Anchor

57. In which year did it become compulsory to wear seat belts in the front seat of a car in the UK?
  ⌐⌐ 1973
  ⌐⌐ 1983
  ⌐⌐ 1993

58. The bookmaker Bernie Bernbaum and the gangster Tom Regan are characters in which Coen Brothers film?
  ⌐⌐ Blood Simple
  ⌐⌐ Fargo
  ⌐⌐ Miller's Crossing

59. Which bingo number is referred to as 'Fat lady with a crutch'?
  ⌐⌐ 87
  ⌐⌐ 57
  ⌐⌐ 27

60. Jerry Garcia was the guitarist of which influential US band?
  ⌐⌐ The Eagles
  ⌐⌐ The Grateful Dead
  ⌐⌐ The Byrds

ANSWERS ON P.274

61. The advice to actors, 'Just say the lines and don't trip over the furniture' is attributed to which playwright?
- ⊔ Noël Coward
- ⊔ John Osborne
- ⊔ Harold Pinter

62. Mr and Mrs Gardiner are the aunt and uncle of which Jane Austen heroine?
- ⊔ Elinor Dashwood
- ⊔ Fanny Price
- ⊔ Elizabeth Bennet

63. In nautical terms, a barrelman would traditionally be found in which part of the ship?
- ⊔ Crow's Nest
- ⊔ Poop Deck
- ⊔ Quarter Gallery

64. In 1979, who became the first Western rock star to play in the old Soviet Union?
- ⊔ John Lennon
- ⊔ Elton John
- ⊔ Sting

65. From which part of an animal is 'tripe' made?
- ⊔ Stomach
- ⊔ Brains
- ⊔ Tongue

66. Which comic strip character is famous for eating cow-pies with the horns left in?
- ⊔ Desperate Dan
- ⊔ Dennis the Menace
- ⊔ Minnie the Minx

ANSWERS ON P.274

67. According to the saying, what does familiarity breed?
- ⊔ Dislike
- ⊔ Contempt
- ⊔ Neglect

68. What name was given to the European travels undertaken by young Englishmen of rank in the 17th and 18th centuries?
- ⊔ The Long Trek
- ⊔ The Great Walk
- ⊔ The Grand Tour

69. The musk ox is native to which region?
- ⊔ Arctic
- ⊔ Sahara
- ⊔ Himalayas

70. The medieval 'Lewis chessmen', now mostly in the British Museum, were discovered in which country in the 19th century?
- ⊔ Wales
- ⊔ Scotland
- ⊔ Northern Ireland

71. In terms of area, what is the smallest country in the European Union?
- ⊔ Finland
- ⊔ Belgium
- ⊔ Malta

72. Which former All Saints singer married Oasis frontman Liam Gallagher on Valentine's Day in 2008?
- ⊔ Melanie Blatt
- ⊔ Shaznay Lewis
- ⊔ Nicole Appleton

ANSWERS ON P.274

73. In which year did China implement its 'one child per couple' policy?
- ⊔ 1960
- ⊔ 1970
- ⊔ 1980

74. How old was Mary, Queen of Scots when she succeeded to the throne on the death of her father?
- ⊔ Six Days
- ⊔ Six Years
- ⊔ Sixteen Years

75. In the military, what name is given to a small case for needles, thread and other small sewing items?
- ⊔ Housewife
- ⊔ Chambermaid
- ⊔ Governess

76. Which prison is featured in John Gay's work *The Beggar's Opera*?
- ⊔ Wormwood Scrubs
- ⊔ Fleet
- ⊔ Newgate

77. Who is the father of daughters called Fifi Trixiebelle, Peaches and Pixie?
- ⊔ Brad Pitt
- ⊔ Bruce Willis
- ⊔ Bob Geldof

78. In 1977, who became the first woman to be nominated for a Best Director Oscar?
- ⊔ Sally Potter
- ⊔ Lina Wertmuller
- ⊔ Allison Anders

ANSWERS ON P.274

79. In which year did the Soviet Union pull its last troops out of Afghanistan?
    - 1969
    - 1979
    - 1989

80. Which word, derived from the Greek for 'bad', means government by the worst people?
    - Kakistocracy
    - Malistocracy
    - Daemonocracy

81. Who was the original host of the TV cooking show *MasterChef*?
    - Ainsley Harriott
    - Loyd Grossman
    - Jamie Oliver

82. In terms of volume, a standard tablespoon is equal to how many teaspoons?
    - 1
    - 3
    - 9

83. What is the name of the 2,800-acre Californian ranch, bought by Michael Jackson in 1988?
    - Narnia
    - Neverland
    - The Magic Kingdom

84. Which British actor, who starred in the 1997 film *Nil By Mouth*, won 80 of his 88 fights as an amateur welterweight boxer?
    - Ray Winstone
    - Sean Bean
    - Rhys Ifans

ANSWERS ON P.274

85. What does the Latin phrase 'Dei Gratia' mean?
- ⌴ By the Grace of God
- ⌴ Fall from Grace
- ⌴ Saving Grace

86. In the Bible, which sense does Saul lose on the road to Damascus?
- ⌴ Smell
- ⌴ Hearing
- ⌴ Sight

87. Which word describes the practice of creating and reading codes?
- ⌴ Cartography
- ⌴ Chrysology
- ⌴ Cryptology

88. What does a person suffering from hypersomnia tend to do a lot?
- ⌴ Eat
- ⌴ Sleep
- ⌴ Talk

89. In Norse mythology, what name is given to the handmaidens who served the gods?
- ⌴ Valkyries
- ⌴ Sirens
- ⌴ Harpies

90. An alembic is used in which process for making alcoholic beverages?
- ⌴ Brewing
- ⌴ Winemaking
- ⌴ Distilling

ANSWERS ON P.274

91. What kind of institution is a 'Bourse'?
- ⨆ Medical Centre
- ⨆ Ballet School
- ⨆ Stock Exchange

92. What word derives from a Scots golfing term describing a situation where a shot is blocked by an opponent's ball?
- ⨆ Banjax
- ⨆ Stymie
- ⨆ Balk

93. In which activity is the 'Ben Day process' a widely used technique?
- ⨆ Singing
- ⨆ Printing
- ⨆ Food Preservation

94. Which dish, popular in the southern United States, is made from coarsely ground corn?
- ⨆ Grits
- ⨆ Jambalaya
- ⨆ Smores

95. What type of foodstuff is coley?
- ⨆ Vegetable
- ⨆ Fish
- ⨆ Fruit

96. Which London square gave its name to the upper middle classes who traditionally live in West London?
- ⨆ Eaton Square
- ⨆ Berkeley Square
- ⨆ Sloane Square

ANSWERS ON P.274

97. In which game do the marbles or pegs have to be
successively captured until only one is left?
- ⊔ Cribbage
- ⊔ Solitaire
- ⊔ Othello

98. Which supermarket founder had the motto 'pile 'em high,
sell 'em cheap'?
- ⊔ Jack Cohen
- ⊔ John James Sainsbury
- ⊔ William Morrison

99. Which country's national anthem has been without official
lyrics since 1978?
- ⊔ Germany
- ⊔ Spain
- ⊔ Chile

100. Who is the Greek god of wine?
- ⊔ Dionysus
- ⊔ Hephaestus
- ⊔ Poseidon

ANSWERS ON P.274

JUDITH KEPPEL

FULL NAME:
Judith Keppel

HOME TOWN:
London

EDUCATION:
7 different schools; 8 O-levels, 2 A-levels, History of Art degree at University College London.

QUIZZING CREDS:
1st winner of £1,000,000 on *Who Wants to Be a Millionaire?*

LEAST FAVOURITE SUBJECT:
Sport

SPECIAL INTEREST:
I am interested in everything except sport.

WHAT DOES IT TAKE TO BE AN EGGHEAD:
A good memory and curiosity.

WHO WOULD BE ON YOUR ULTIMATE FANTASY QUIZ TEAM:
Benjamin Franklin (polymath); Leonardo da Vinci (Science and Art); Georges Auguste Escoffier (Food and Drink); Sir Francis Drake (Geography); Benjamin Disraeli (History, Politics, Literature); Clare Balding (Sport); Sam Delaney (ex-editor of *Heat* Magazine).

MEMORABLE MOMENT:
I won a Politics round against Edwina Currie and a Science round against a rocket scientist.

ADVICE FOR BUDDING EGGHEAD:
Read the papers.

MY FAVOURITE PIECE OF TRIVIA:
What kind of a creature is a Sarcastic Fringehead? (Killer Question 29, in this book).

LITTLE KNOWN FACT ABOUT YOU:
Aged ten in Damascus, I wanted to buy a dagger so wandered off alone into the souk and was later found by my frantic parents bargaining with a stallholder. I still have the dagger.

1. In the children's book *The Very Hungry Caterpillar*, what is the first thing the caterpillar eats?
   - ⌴ Banana
   - ⌴ Strawberry
   - ⌴ Apple

2. Before moving to the South Bank, where was the National Theatre based?
   - ⌴ Barbican
   - ⌴ Old Vic
   - ⌴ Theatre Royal Haymarket

3. The plot of Shakespeare's *All's Well That Ends Well* is derived from a story found in which earlier work?
   - ⌴ The Canterbury Tales
   - ⌴ The Divine Comedy
   - ⌴ The Decameron

4. Which painter, who died in 1906, is quoted as saying 'I will astonish Paris with an apple'?
   - ⌴ Paul Cézanne
   - ⌴ Pablo Picasso
   - ⌴ Edgar Degas

5. Who wrote the plays *The Father* and *The Dance of Death*?
   - ⌴ Ibsen
   - ⌴ Chekhov
   - ⌴ Strindberg

6. Which Algerian city is the setting for the novel *The Plague* by Albert Camus?
   - ⌴ Médéa
   - ⌴ Algiers
   - ⌴ Oran

ANSWERS ON P.275

7. A diluted layer of watercolour spread on a painting is known as a what?
   - ⊔ Wash
   - ⊔ Scrub
   - ⊔ Buff

8. Which playwright is known as the 'Bard of Avon'?
   - ⊔ Christopher Marlowe
   - ⊔ Ben Jonson
   - ⊔ William Shakespeare

9. Who is the narrator of Ken Kesey's novel *One Flew Over the Cuckoo's Nest*?
   - ⊔ Dale Harding
   - ⊔ Doctor Spivey
   - ⊔ Chief Bromden

10. Who painted the 1856 portrait entitled *Madame Moitessier*, which is part of the collection of the National Gallery in London?
    - ⊔ Monet
    - ⊔ Ingres
    - ⊔ Vermeer

11. Thomas Hobbes's book *Behemoth* is an investigation into the causes of which historical episode?
    - ⊔ English Civil Wars
    - ⊔ Great Fire of London
    - ⊔ Colonisation of America

12. The 1914 book of prose poems entitled *Tender Buttons* is a work by which writer?
    - ⊔ Hilda Doolittle
    - ⊔ Virginia Woolf
    - ⊔ Gertrude Stein

ANSWERS ON P.275

13. In Patricia Cornwell's series of crime novels, what is the occupation of Kay Scarpetta?
    ⊔ Private Nurse
    ⊔ Medical Examiner
    ⊔ Pharmacist

14. L.S. Lowry's famous painting *Going to the Match* shows a crowd of fans on their way to the ground of which football team?
    ⊔ Queens Park Rangers
    ⊔ Bolton Wanderers
    ⊔ Bristol Rovers

15. In *Great Expectations* by Charles Dickens, who does Pip's love Estella marry?
    ⊔ Matthew Pocket
    ⊔ John Wemmick
    ⊔ Bentley Drummle

16. What is the name of the Theatre Cat in T.S. Eliot's *Old Possum's Book of Practical Cats*?
    ⊔ Griff
    ⊔ Glenda
    ⊔ Gus

17. To which seaside town, home to his great-aunt Betsey, does David Copperfield run when he leaves London?
    ⊔ Dover
    ⊔ Skegness
    ⊔ Weymouth

18. Which English comedic actor wrote the 2010 autobiography *Nerd Do Well*?
    ⊔ Martin Freeman
    ⊔ Russell Brand
    ⊔ Simon Pegg

ANSWERS ON P.275

19. The twins Pat and Isobel O'Sullivan are central characters in a series of books by Enid Blyton featuring which boarding school?
- ⌴ St Clare's
- ⌴ St Eleanor's
- ⌴ St Bernadette's

20. Which Shakespeare play features foolish servants called Speed and Launce?
- ⌴ The Merry Wives of Windsor
- ⌴ The Two Gentlemen of Verona
- ⌴ All's Well That Ends Well

21. Which artist won the 2010 Turner Prize for a sound installation that featured her own voice?
- ⌴ Gillian Wearing
- ⌴ Susan Philipsz
- ⌴ Angela de la Cruz

22. Olga, Masha and Irina are the names of the sisters in which play?
- ⌴ King Lear
- ⌴ Three Sisters
- ⌴ A Woman of No Importance

23. Who wrote the 2010 novel *A Tiny Bit Marvellous*?
- ⌴ Dawn French
- ⌴ Miranda Hart
- ⌴ Kathy Burke

24. Who wrote the 1920s novel *All Quiet on the Western Front*?
- ⌴ Erich Maria Remarque
- ⌴ Willi Heinrich
- ⌴ Hans Fallada

ANSWERS ON P.275

25. Great Uncle Bulgaria is seen as the head of which group of fictional characters?
- ⌣ The Borrowers
- ⌣ The Moomins
- ⌣ The Wombles

26. What mode of dress is most associated with the artists Gilbert and George?
- ⌣ Suits
- ⌣ Kilts
- ⌣ Wellingtons

27. Found on antiques, picture frames and furniture, what type of finish is 'ormolu'?
- ⌣ Distressed Leather
- ⌣ Painted Wood
- ⌣ Gilded Bronze

28. Which broadcaster and former MP has written a series of books known collectively as the *Oscar Wilde Murder Mysteries*?
- ⌣ Austin Mitchell
- ⌣ Gyles Brandreth
- ⌣ Matthew Parris

29. The Djanogly Art Gallery is in which British city?
- ⌣ Leicester
- ⌣ Nottingham
- ⌣ Derby

30. Sir Fopling Flutter is a character in which Restoration comedy?
- ⌣ The Beaux' Stratagem
- ⌣ The Recruiting Officer
- ⌣ The Man of Mode

ANSWERS ON P.275

31. The term 'quattrocento' is used to refer to Italian art of which century?
- ⌐⌐ 3rd Century
- ⌐⌐ 15th Century
- ⌐⌐ 20th Century

32. The word 'limner' refers to which type of artist?
- ⌐⌐ Photographer
- ⌐⌐ Sculptor
- ⌐⌐ Painter

33. The character Maura Ryan, queen of London's Underworld, was created by which writer?
- ⌐⌐ Lynda La Plante
- ⌐⌐ Martina Cole
- ⌐⌐ Kate Atkinson

34. What was the title of Stephenie Meyer's first published sequel to her novel *Twilight*?
- ⌐⌐ Crescent Moon
- ⌐⌐ New Moon
- ⌐⌐ Harvest Moon

35. The book subtitled *First Step 2 Forever: My Story* is the first book by which popstar?
- ⌐⌐ Miley Cyrus
- ⌐⌐ Joe McElderry
- ⌐⌐ Justin Bieber

36. Which artist, who died in 1920, was noted for his portraits depicting people with mask-like faces and elongated figures?
- ⌐⌐ Mondrian
- ⌐⌐ Modigliani
- ⌐⌐ Magritte

ANSWERS ON P.275

37. How many people are depicted in the diner in Edward Hopper's painting *Nighthawks*?
- ⌴ 12
- ⌴ 7
- ⌴ 4

38. The actress Maud Gonne inspired many poems by which writer?
- ⌴ W.B. Yeats
- ⌴ Algernon Swinburne
- ⌴ Rupert Brooke

39. The writer Madeleine Wickham has also published novels under what name?
- ⌴ Marian Keyes
- ⌴ Helen Fielding
- ⌴ Sophie Kinsella

40. In the books by P.D. James, Adam Dalgliesh is well-known for doing what apart from policing?
- ⌴ Writing Poetry
- ⌴ Making Quilts
- ⌴ Baking Bread

41. In the early days of Penguin paperbacks, mystery and crime novels were associated with what sleeve colour?
- ⌴ Green
- ⌴ Orange
- ⌴ Brown

42. Edward Murdstone is the stepfather of which Dickens character?
- ⌴ Oliver Twist
- ⌴ David Copperfield
- ⌴ Little Nell

ANSWERS ON P.275

43. *If Only They Could Talk* and *It Shouldn't Happen To a Vet* are books published under which writer's name?
- ⊔ Terry Nutkins
- ⊔ Trude Mostue
- ⊔ James Herriot

44. Which Irish playwright's home in Ayot St Lawrence in Hertfordshire has been preserved as he left it by the National Trust?
- ⊔ Sean O'Casey
- ⊔ George Bernard Shaw
- ⊔ Oliver Goldsmith

45. What is the profession of the character Lew Archer in the series of novels by the writer Ross Macdonald?
- ⊔ Newspaper Editor
- ⊔ Private Detective
- ⊔ Big Game Hunter

46. In typography, what name is given to any part of a lower case letter that extends below the baseline?
- ⊔ Descender
- ⊔ Dropper
- ⊔ Deposer

47. Which 19th-century muse famously posed as Ophelia in the painting of the same name by John Everett Millais?
- ⊔ Effie Gray
- ⊔ Elizabeth Siddal
- ⊔ Jane Burden

48. 'Treen' is the name given to simple household objects made out of what material?
- ⊔ Tin
- ⊔ Cotton
- ⊔ Wood

ANSWERS ON P.275

49. Which 19th-century novel is subtitled 'The Autobiography of a Horse'?
- ⌴ Black Beauty
- ⌴ National Velvet
- ⌴ Follyfoot

50. The Booker Prize-winning author Peter Carey was born in which country?
- ⌴ Canada
- ⌴ Australia
- ⌴ Republic of Ireland

51. 'How sharper than a serpent's tooth it is to have a thankless child!' is a line from which Shakespeare play?
- ⌴ Hamlet
- ⌴ Antony and Cleopatra
- ⌴ King Lear

52. Which was the first of James Patterson's novels to feature Alex Cross?
- ⌴ Along Came a Spider
- ⌴ Don't Blink
- ⌴ 4th of July

53. The mural known as *The Aldobrandini Wedding* was painted in which period?
- ⌴ Roman
- ⌴ Renaissance
- ⌴ Rococo

54. Who wrote *A Time of Gifts*, a famous piece of travel-writing published in 1977?
- ⌴ Gavin Maxwell
- ⌴ Patrick Leigh Fermor
- ⌴ Lawrence Durrell

ANSWERS ON P.275

55. The novels *The Body in the Library* and *At Bertram's Hotel* feature which character?
- ⊔ Miss Marple
- ⊔ Kay Scarpetta
- ⊔ Nancy Drew

56. Which best-selling 1998 motivational book was written by Spencer Johnson?
- ⊔ The 4-Hour Workweek
- ⊔ How to Live On 24 Hours a Day
- ⊔ Who Moved My Cheese?

57. Which poet's letters to his lover Monica Jones, who died in 2001, were published in 2010?
- ⊔ Philip Larkin
- ⊔ Thom Gunn
- ⊔ Laurie Lee

58. In 1910, the artist L.S. Lowry began work in which occupation?
- ⊔ Hospital Porter
- ⊔ Rent Collector
- ⊔ Schools Inspector

59. Pat Barker's 1991 novel *Regeneration* centres on which historical conflict?
- ⊔ Wars of the Roses
- ⊔ Napoleonic Wars
- ⊔ World War I

60. What is the surname of the brothers Hal and Roger, who feature in Willard Price's 'Adventure Series' of books?
- ⊔ Hunt
- ⊔ Blackett
- ⊔ Carr

ANSWERS ON P.275

61. Which artist produced the sculpture *Prospero and Ariel* that sits over the entrance to the BBC's Broadcasting House?

⊔ Jacob Epstein
⊔ Henry Moore
⊔ Eric Gill

62. In Hans Christian Andersen's story 'The Tinderbox', the soldier uses the tinderbox to summon which creatures?

⊔ Dogs
⊔ Horses
⊔ Dragons

63. *The First Men in the Moon* is a 1901 science fiction novel by which writer?

⊔ Jules Verne
⊔ J.R.R. Tolkien
⊔ H.G. Wells

64. In Jerome K. Jerome's 1900 sequel to *Three Men in a Boat*, where did the men find themselves?

⊔ On the Bummel
⊔ On a Jaunt
⊔ On Their Uppers

65. Howard Hodgkin is a prize-winning practitioner of which of the arts?

⊔ Poetry
⊔ Painting
⊔ Pottery

66. Which Renaissance painter's works bear the motto 'Als ich chan' or 'As best I can'?

⊔ Jan Van Eyck
⊔ Albrecht Durer
⊔ Hieronymus Bosch

ANSWERS ON P.275

67. In Auguste Rodin's sculpture *The Thinker*, on what is the subject resting his head?
  ⊔ His Knee
  ⊔ His Hand
  ⊔ The Desk

68. What was the title of the first novel by Edgar Rice Burroughs to feature Tarzan?
  ⊔ Tarzan of the Apes
  ⊔ Tarzan of the Lions
  ⊔ Tarzan of the Nile

69. In the book *Alice's Adventures in Wonderland*, who is seated around the tea party table with the Mad Hatter and the Dormouse?
  ⊔ Cheshire Cat
  ⊔ Caterpillar
  ⊔ March Hare

70. In which country was the writer George Orwell born?
  ⊔ Canada
  ⊔ India
  ⊔ New Zealand

71. What term is applied to clay that has had its first firing in a kiln but has not been glazed?
  ⊔ Bisque
  ⊔ Dunt
  ⊔ Pug

72. Which musical instrument takes its name from the Italian for 'small'?
  ⊔ Piccolo
  ⊔ Cello
  ⊔ Recorder

ANSWERS ON P.275

73. *Death of a Naturalist* and *Station Island* are collections of poetry by which writer?
  ⊔ Carol Ann Duffy
  ⊔ Ted Hughes
  ⊔ Seamus Heaney

74. Which arts organisation is based at London's Coliseum?
  ⊔ National Portrait Gallery
  ⊔ English National Opera
  ⊔ National Theatre

75. *Labyrinth* and *Sepulchre* are books by which author?
  ⊔ Kate Mosse
  ⊔ Dan Brown
  ⊔ Patricia Cornwell

76. George Sand produced a book about which Mediterranean island after spending a winter there with Frederic Chopin?
  ⊔ Corsica
  ⊔ Cyprus
  ⊔ Majorca

77. 'The Charge of the Light Brigade' is a poem by which writer?
  ⊔ Wordsworth
  ⊔ Tennyson
  ⊔ Keats

78. *Green Eggs and Ham* is a best-selling children's book by which author?
  ⊔ Dr Seuss
  ⊔ Lewis Carroll
  ⊔ J.R.R. Tolkien

ANSWERS ON P.275

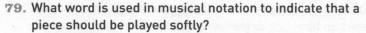

79. What word is used in musical notation to indicate that a piece should be played softly?
- ⊔ Andante
- ⊔ Glissando
- ⊔ Piano

80. Carlos Acosta is a leading name in which field of the arts?
- ⊔ Ballet
- ⊔ Poetry
- ⊔ Sculpture

81. Which Czech composer, who was born in Leitomischl, Bohemia in 1824, wrote the opera *The Bartered Bride*?
- ⊔ Janacek
- ⊔ Dvorak
- ⊔ Smetana

82. In the Shakespeare play *Henry V*, the Battle of Agincourt is fought on which saint's day?
- ⊔ St Anthony
- ⊔ St Jude
- ⊔ St Crispin

83. 'The Thought-Fox' is a poem by which British writer?
- ⊔ Ted Hughes
- ⊔ John Betjeman
- ⊔ Dylan Thomas

84. *The French Lieutenant's Woman* is a novel by which author?
- ⊔ John Fowles
- ⊔ D.H. Lawrence
- ⊔ Robert Graves

ANSWERS ON P.275

85. Of which young composer did Mozart comment, 'Keep your eyes on him; one day he will make the world talk of him'?
   ⊔ Bach
   ⊔ Beethoven
   ⊔ Brahms

86. What gained members of the public admission to Willie Wonka's chocolate factory in the Roald Dahl book?
   ⊔ A Golden Ticket
   ⊔ A Silver Dollar
   ⊔ A Bronze Key

87. Which storyteller, born in 1805, wrote the story of 'The Ugly Duckling'?
   ⊔ Oscar Wilde
   ⊔ Wilhelm Grimm
   ⊔ Hans Christian Andersen

88. 'Drink to me' are reputed to be the last words of which artist?
   ⊔ Pablo Picasso
   ⊔ Salvador Dalí
   ⊔ Joan Miró

89. Which poet does Dante use as his guide through Hell in *The Divine Comedy*?
   ⊔ Homer
   ⊔ Ovid
   ⊔ Virgil

90. In Tolkien's books about Middle Earth, what name is given to the tree creatures of Fangorn Forest?
   ⊔ Dwarves
   ⊔ Orcs
   ⊔ Ents

ANSWERS ON P.275

91. *Appalachian Spring* is a ballet by which composer?
- ⊔ John Cage
- ⊔ Aaron Copland
- ⊔ Benjamin Britten

92. Which literary detective lives in the fictional Sussex town of Kingsmarkham?
- ⊔ Inspector Wexford
- ⊔ Adam Dalgliesh
- ⊔ Hercule Poirot

93. The 19th-century painting known as 'Bubbles', featuring a young boy holding a pipe and a bowl of soapsuds, is by which artist?
- ⊔ Edward Burne-Jones
- ⊔ Ford Madox Brown
- ⊔ John Everett Millais

94. What term is used to refer to a literary work which imitates the style of a particular writer in a humorous way?
- ⊔ Novella
- ⊔ Hyperbole
- ⊔ Parody

95. Which musical term refers to the notes of a chord played upward or downward in quick succession?
- ⊔ Lento
- ⊔ Vibrato
- ⊔ Arpeggio

96. The line 'The rule is, jam to-morrow and jam yesterday – but never jam to-day' appears in a book by which author?
- ⊔ Charles Dickens
- ⊔ Jane Austen
- ⊔ Lewis Carroll

ANSWERS ON P.275

97. Who wrote the 1989 novel *A Year in Provence* which was made into a TV series starring John Thaw and Lindsay Duncan?
  ⊔ Nigel Barley
  ⊔ Peter Mayle
  ⊔ Graham Greene

98. The elaborately decorated cream-coloured pottery called 'Satsuma ware' was originally produced in which country?
  ⊔ Greece
  ⊔ Japan
  ⊔ Russia

99. Ashley Wilkes and Melanie Hamilton are supporting characters in which American novel, published in 1936?
  ⊔ Little Women
  ⊔ The Catcher in the Rye
  ⊔ Gone With the Wind

100. The cottage on the River Stour featured in John Constable's painting *The Hay Wain* is described as belonging to whom?
  ⊔ Willy Lott
  ⊔ Kitty Scott
  ⊔ Freddy Trott

ANSWERS ON P.275

1. What does the Latin phrase 'Vivat Regina' mean?
   ⌣ Live and Let Die
   ⌣ Live Long and Prosper
   ⌣ Long Live the Queen

2. Which creatures are described as 'educated' in the lyrics to Cole Porter's song 'Let's Do It (Let's Fall In Love)'?
   ⌣ Frogs
   ⌣ Fish
   ⌣ Fleas

3. Which region is located at the 'toe' of the so-called boot of Italy?
   ⌣ Campania
   ⌣ Calabria
   ⌣ Tuscany

4. What was the name of the Queen Consort of King Edward VII?
   ⌣ Alexandra
   ⌣ Laurentien
   ⌣ Christina

5. In Greek mythology, Achilles was the son of the king of which people?
   ⌣ Spartans
   ⌣ Achaeans
   ⌣ Myrmidons

6. Which actress married Al Jolson in 1928?
   ⌣ Ruby Keeler
   ⌣ Mildred Davis
   ⌣ Bebe Daniels

ANSWERS ON P.276

7. Who designed and sculpted the statue of Nelson on the top of Nelson's Column in Trafalgar Square?
   - ⊔ Walter Gilbert
   - ⊔ John Henry Foley
   - ⊔ Edward H. Baily

8. In which present-day country was the cosmetics entrepreneur known as Max Factor born in 1877?
   - ⊔ Poland
   - ⊔ France
   - ⊔ Germany

9. In which American state is the university known by the initials 'UCLA' located?
   - ⊔ California
   - ⊔ Louisiana
   - ⊔ Alabama

10. 'Stingo' is a particularly strong type of which drink?
   - ⊔ Cider
   - ⊔ Whisky
   - ⊔ Beer

11. What is the common name for the plant genus 'myosotis'?
   - ⊔ Forget-Me-Not
   - ⊔ Carnation
   - ⊔ Laburnum

12. Which alcoholic spirit is the base of the cocktail known as a Pimms No. 1 Cup?
   - ⊔ Gin
   - ⊔ Whisky
   - ⊔ Tequila

ANSWERS ON P.276

13. In Puccini's opera *Turandot*, what is the name of the
character who sings the aria 'Nessun Dorma'?
  ⌴ Altoum
  ⌴ Parpignol
  ⌴ Calaf

14. What is the title of Izaak Walton's classic 1653 book,
subtitled 'The Contemplative Man's Recreation'?
  ⌴ The Compleat Hunter
  ⌴ The Compleat Gardener
  ⌴ The Compleat Angler

15. The Camp David Agreements of 1978–9 were a series of
accords agreed between which two countries?
  ⌴ India and Pakistan
  ⌴ Israel and Egypt
  ⌴ USA and China

16. For what does the letter 'C' stand in the abbreviation of the
international organisation of industrialised countries the
OECD?
  ⌴ Common
  ⌴ Council
  ⌴ Co-operation

17. Which company launched the first ever credit card in New
York in 1950?
  ⌴ American Express
  ⌴ Visa
  ⌴ Diners Club

18. For what does the letter 'M' stand in the government
abbreviation 'MI5'?
  ⌴ Military
  ⌴ Mission
  ⌴ Mainland

ANSWERS ON P.276

19. The village of Beaulieu, famous for the National Motor Museum, is located in which English National Park?
- ⎵ Peak District
- ⎵ Exmoor
- ⎵ New Forest

20. In Greek mythology, Athena, the goddess of war, emerged fully grown from the forehead of which God?
- ⎵ Apollo
- ⎵ Zeus
- ⎵ Hermes

21. Richard Nixon and which other US president were born in 1913?
- ⎵ Gerald Ford
- ⎵ John F. Kennedy
- ⎵ Ronald Reagan

22. Which part of the body is sometimes informally referred to as the 'fizzog'?
- ⎵ Stomach
- ⎵ Face
- ⎵ Legs

23. In which country did Elvis Presley spend his military service, from October 1958 to March 1960?
- ⎵ West Germany
- ⎵ Poland
- ⎵ Mexico

24. Which popular website was co-founded by Mark Zuckerberg while he was a student at Harvard University?
- ⎵ Facebook
- ⎵ Wikipedia
- ⎵ MySpace

ANSWERS ON P.276

25. Which character was played by Harrison Ford in the 1977 film *Star Wars*?

  ⌣ Han Solo
  ⌣ Luke Skywalker
  ⌣ Darth Vader

26. Which apparent aid to the regulation of traffic was invented by former rally driver Maurice Gatsonides in the 1950s?

  ⌣ Speed Camera
  ⌣ Traffic Lights
  ⌣ Satellite Navigation

27. Korčula, Hvar and Krk are islands lying off the west coast of which European country?

  ⌣ Croatia
  ⌣ Greece
  ⌣ Turkey

28. Who won a Best Supporting Actress Oscar for her performance in the 1988 film *The Accidental Tourist*?

  ⌣ Geena Davis
  ⌣ Sally Field
  ⌣ Jessica Lange

29. From 1948 to 1960, Syngman Rhee was president of which country?

  ⌣ South Korea
  ⌣ India
  ⌣ Philippines

30. Which car company is famous for producing the Phantom and Silver Shadow models?

  ⌣ Jaguar
  ⌣ Rolls Royce
  ⌣ Morris

ANSWERS ON P.276

31. Who made his film debut as Clint Reno in *Love Me Tender* in 1956?
- ⏟ Frank Sinatra
- ⏟ Sammy Davis Jnr
- ⏟ Elvis Presley

32. Touchstone the Jester is a character in which Shakespeare play?
- ⏟ Macbeth
- ⏟ As You Like It
- ⏟ Othello

33. Which US city was ravaged in 1871 by a Great Fire that burned for days and left thousands homeless?
- ⏟ New York
- ⏟ San Francisco
- ⏟ Chicago

34. 'Matelot' is an old-fashioned slang word for which kind of serviceman?
- ⏟ Soldier
- ⏟ Pilot
- ⏟ Sailor

35. Which Roman emperor is said to have boasted that 'he found Rome a city of brick and left it a city of marble'?
- ⏟ Augustus
- ⏟ Nero
- ⏟ Vespasian

36. What breed of dog was the film star Rin Tin Tin?
- ⏟ German Shepherd
- ⏟ Dalmatian
- ⏟ Golden Retriever

ANSWERS ON P.276

37. Which language is believed to have been spoken by Jesus and the Apostles?
- ⊔ Latin
- ⊔ Greek
- ⊔ Aramaic

38. How many women were there in the 2002 BBC Top 100 Greatest Britons list, of which Winston Churchill came top?
- ⊔ 3
- ⊔ 13
- ⊔ 33

39. The football team Atalanta is based in which Italian city?
- ⊔ Bergamo
- ⊔ Milan
- ⊔ Genoa

40. Which cathedral city lends its name to a low open-topped cabinet with partitions for holding music or books?
- ⊔ Canterbury
- ⊔ Winchester
- ⊔ Salisbury

41. A Torr is a unit of measurement for what?
- ⊔ Resistance
- ⊔ Length
- ⊔ Pressure

42. Which fictional character lives with his friends in 'Hundred Acre Wood'?
- ⊔ Paddington Bear
- ⊔ Winnie-the-Pooh
- ⊔ Yogi Bear

ANSWERS ON P.276

43. The Shtreimel is a type of hat worn by male members of which faith?
    - ⊔ Judaism
    - ⊔ Islam
    - ⊔ Christianity

44. What type of creature is a shubunkin?
    - ⊔ Snake
    - ⊔ Fish
    - ⊔ Bird

45. 'Tis better to be brief than tedious' is a line from which Shakespeare play?
    - ⊔ Macbeth
    - ⊔ Hamlet
    - ⊔ Richard III

46. The portrait of which American President is printed on the front of a US dollar bill?
    - ⊔ George Washington
    - ⊔ Abraham Lincoln
    - ⊔ Thomas Jefferson

47. What word of Yiddish origin refers to the stage routine of a stand-up comedian?
    - ⊔ Schmuck
    - ⊔ Schmaltz
    - ⊔ Shtick

48. What name is given to any language that is used as a means of communication between speakers of different native languages?
    - ⊔ Lingua Anglica
    - ⊔ Lingua Franca
    - ⊔ Lingua Germania

ANSWERS ON P.276

49. The French city of Limoges is famous for the production of what?
- ⊔ Ironwork
- ⊔ Porcelain
- ⊔ Glass

50. What normally runs through a ship's hawsepipes?
- ⊔ Fuel Oil
- ⊔ Compressed Air
- ⊔ Anchor Cable

51. During World War II, Karl Dönitz was in charge of which aspect of Germany's military machine?
- ⊔ Bombers
- ⊔ Submarines
- ⊔ Tanks

52. What name is sometimes given to the tops of ocean waves in particularly choppy weather?
- ⊔ White Monkeys
- ⊔ White Tigers
- ⊔ White Horses

53. 'Numpty' is an affectionate Scottish term for what?
- ⊔ Child
- ⊔ Idiot
- ⊔ Husband

54. What type of animal is the Teenage Mutant Ninja Turtles' father-figure Master Splinter?
- ⊔ Mutant Frog
- ⊔ Mutant Rat
- ⊔ Mutant Alligator

ANSWERS ON P.276

55. Which car manufacturer produced the 'Testarossa'?
- ⊔ Ferrari
- ⊔ Lotus
- ⊔ Porsche

56. Which telecommunications company was founded by Akio Morita and Masaru Ibuka in 1946?
- ⊔ Time Warner
- ⊔ Sony
- ⊔ MGM

57. The Oscar-winning actor Javier Bardem played international rugby for which country as a teenager?
- ⊔ Argentina
- ⊔ Spain
- ⊔ Uruguay

58. Which organisation was founded by Dr Chad Varah in 1953?
- ⊔ Samaritans
- ⊔ Red Cross
- ⊔ Amnesty International

59. According to the Bible, who was forced to help Jesus carry his cross to his execution?
- ⊔ Simon of Cyrene
- ⊔ Barabbas
- ⊔ Joseph Caiaphas

60. The BND is the federal intelligence agency of which national government?
- ⊔ France
- ⊔ Germany
- ⊔ Italy

ANSWERS ON P.276

61. What is usually missing on true Manx cats?
- ⌐ Ears
- ⌐ Tail
- ⌐ Claws

62. Which product was introduced into the UK in 1960 and marketed through parties held in people's homes?
- ⌐ Electrolux Vacuum Cleaners
- ⌐ Avon Cosmetics
- ⌐ Tupperware

63. In 1986, 'The Chicken Song' was a UK number one hit single for characters from which TV show?
- ⌐ The Wombles
- ⌐ Spitting Image
- ⌐ Grange Hill

64. What title is given to daughters of the Spanish sovereign?
- ⌐ Infanta
- ⌐ Bambina
- ⌐ Hermana

65. Mount Carmel is a high ridge that shelters which modern port?
- ⌐ Haifa
- ⌐ Piraeus
- ⌐ Tripoli

66. What is the cube root of 512?
- ⌐ 8
- ⌐ 12
- ⌐ 16

ANSWERS ON P.276

67. In sport, a 'varsity' match is a competition between teams from what type of establishments?
- ⊔ Police Forces
- ⊔ Universities
- ⊔ Churches

68. What type of transport is the Canadian 'komatik'?
- ⊔ Sledge
- ⊔ Canoe
- ⊔ Tricycle

69. The Vizsla is a breed of dog originally from which country?
- ⊔ Russia
- ⊔ Greece
- ⊔ Hungary

70. The 'briny' is another name for what?
- ⊔ Sky
- ⊔ Countryside
- ⊔ Sea

71. In 1959, the Dalai Lama's Government was exiled to which country?
- ⊔ Vietnam
- ⊔ India
- ⊔ Bangladesh

72. What nickname was given to a boy on a ship employed to carry kegs to the gunners?
- ⊔ Powder Monkey
- ⊔ Loblolly Boy
- ⊔ Purser

ANSWERS ON P.276

73. Brian Redhead regularly presented which radio programme between 1975 and 1994?
- From Our Own Correspondent
- Today
- The World at One

74. Who plays the title role in the 2008 film *Iron Man*?
- Ben Affleck
- Robert Downey Jnr
- Hugh Jackman

75. On a Spanish Tapas menu, what food is referred to as 'gambas'?
- Potatoes
- Ham
- Prawns

76. Michaela Tabb is a leading official in which sport?
- Cricket
- Snooker
- Football

77. In Japan, 'Shinobi' is another name for a what?
- Temple
- Kimono
- Ninja

78. Leatherback, flatback and olive ridley are all varieties of which creature?
- Seal
- Jellyfish
- Turtle

ANSWERS ON P.276

79. What was the name of the diary secretary who admitted in 2006 that she had had a two year affair with John Prescott?
- ⊔ Sara Keays
- ⊔ Anna Cox
- ⊔ Tracey Temple

80. Springfield is the capital of which US state?
- ⊔ Colorado
- ⊔ Oklahoma
- ⊔ Illinois

81. What was the nationality of theologian and philosopher Søren Kierkegaard?
- ⊔ Danish
- ⊔ Norwegian
- ⊔ Swedish

82. Cornelius Drebbel invented one of the first examples of what in 1620?
- ⊔ Submarine
- ⊔ Rubber Band
- ⊔ Barometer

83. What would you normally do in a refectory?
- ⊔ Eat
- ⊔ Fight
- ⊔ Wash

84. What is the only film directed by Alfred Hitchcock that won the Academy Award for Best Picture?
- ⊔ North by Northwest
- ⊔ Psycho
- ⊔ Rebecca

ANSWERS ON P.276

85. Maputo is the capital of which country?
└┘ Swaziland
└┘ Mozambique
└┘ Morocco

86. The island of Murano, north of Venice, is most associated with which industry?
└┘ Glassblowing
└┘ Winemaking
└┘ Shipbuilding

87. On which part of the body are 'barrettes' normally worn?
└┘ Feet
└┘ Hands
└┘ Head

88. Odie is the name of a pet dog in which American comic strip?
└┘ Garfield
└┘ Peanuts
└┘ Calvin and Hobbes

89. In which city is Robert Gordon university based?
└┘ Liverpool
└┘ Aberdeen
└┘ Belfast

90. 'Cubby' Broccoli is most notable as a producer of which series of films?
└┘ James Bond
└┘ Star Wars
└┘ Carry On

ANSWERS ON P.276

91. Vaulting is ornamental work normally seen on what part of a building?
- ⌴ Floor
- ⌴ Wall
- ⌴ Ceiling

92. Who is the author of the novels *Enigma* and *Pompeii*?
- ⌴ Robert Graves
- ⌴ Robert Ludlum
- ⌴ Robert Harris

93. What name is given to the narrow inlet of the Bosphorus that divides Istanbul and forms a natural harbour?
- ⌴ Silver Horn
- ⌴ Golden Horn
- ⌴ Steel Horn

94. What is the capital of the Indian state of Tamil Nadu?
- ⌴ Chennai
- ⌴ Bangalore
- ⌴ Hyderabad

95. What is the surname of the British singer usually known only as 'Adele'?
- ⌴ Adamson
- ⌴ Adkins
- ⌴ Appleby

96. In which year did the scientist Alexander Fleming die?
- ⌴ 1915
- ⌴ 1935
- ⌴ 1955

ANSWERS ON P.276

97. Which fast dance, usually performed with the dancers' stomachs touching, takes its name from the Portuguese for 'beating'?
    ⏄ Merengue
    ⏄ Mambo
    ⏄ Lambada

98. Kersey is a type of what?
    ⏄ Cheese
    ⏄ Cloth
    ⏄ Language

99. Which star of black and white movies was known to his friends and family as 'Babe'?
    ⏄ Oliver Hardy
    ⏄ Buster Keaton
    ⏄ Charlie Chaplin

100. In 1961, who became the first person to turn down an invitation to appear on the TV show *This Is Your Life*?
    ⏄ Bill Oddie
    ⏄ Danny Blanchflower
    ⏄ Richard Gordon

ANSWERS ON P.276

DAVID RAINFORD

FULL NAME:
David Omatayo Rainford

HOME TOWN:
Manchester

EDUCATION:
Manchester Grammar School and Parrswood High School.

QUIZZING CREDENTIALS:
Won £250,000 on *Who Wants to Be a Millionaire?*, Semi-finalist and Quarter Finalist on *Are You an Egghead*?

LEAST FAVOURITE SUBJECT:
Anything except Sport!

SPECIAL INTEREST:
Football and cricket.

HOBBIES:
Watching sport.

WHAT DOES IT TAKE TO BE AN EGGHEAD:
Seriously, a broad general knowledge and an ability to face up to anything that is thrown at you.

WHO WOULD BE ON YOUR ULTIMATE FANTASY QUIZ TEAM:
Roy Keane, Clive Lloyd, Susan Sarandon, Martyn Ware and Barbra Streisand.

MOST MEMORABLE MOMENT DURING YOUR TIME AS AN EGGHEAD:
Getting a question wrong where the answer was David, which meant I got knocked out by someone called Dave!

WHAT ADVICE DO YOU HAVE FOR ANY BUDDING EGGHEADS:
Read a lot and absorb as much information as you can. Take part in as many quizzes as you can, so that you can test your knowledge and work on the weaker areas.

WHAT IS YOUR FAVOURITE FACT/ PIECE OF TRIVIA:
Olivia Newton-John is the granddaughter of a Nobel Prize-winning physicist.

LITTLE KNOWN FACT ABOUT YOU:
I got married in Australia.

1. The anthem known as 'Bread of Heaven' is traditionally sung by supporters of which country at Rugby Union matches?
   - Scotland
   - Wales
   - New Zealand

2. In which US sport is a so-called 'designated hitter' employed?
   - Baseball
   - American Football
   - Basketball

3. Where was the legendary welterweight boxer José 'Mantequilla' Napoles born in 1940?
   - Brazil
   - Cuba
   - Panama

4. Which rower, who died in 1977, competed for Great Britain at five Olympic Games, winning three gold and two silver medals?
   - John Kelly
   - Guy Nickalls
   - Jack Beresford

5. Which tennis player did Briton Ann Jones defeat in 1969 to win the Wimbledon Ladies Singles title?
   - Billie Jean King
   - Maria Bueno
   - Evonne Goolagong

6. Square cut, forward drive and sweep are all terms used in which sport?
   - Cricket
   - Tennis
   - Golf

ANSWERS ON P.277

7. In which year did an eighteen-year-old Michael Owen score a stunning solo goal against Argentina in the Football World Cup?
   - ⊔ 1994
   - ⊔ 1998
   - ⊔ 2002

8. 'The Cabbage Patch' is an affectionate nickname for which English sporting venue?
   - ⊔ Lord's
   - ⊔ Twickenham
   - ⊔ Wembley

9. In the mid-1990s, which revolutionary new ski, slim in the middle and wider at each end, appeared for the first time?
   - ⊔ Carving
   - ⊔ Slicing
   - ⊔ Chopping

10. Which British gymnast won a bronze medal in the pommel horse final at the 2007 World Gymnastics Championships in Stuttgart?
    - ⊔ Louis Smith
    - ⊔ Neil Thomas
    - ⊔ Daniel Keatings

11. By what initials is the governing body for tennis in the UK commonly known?
    - ⊔ ETA
    - ⊔ PTA
    - ⊔ LTA

12. Guus Hiddink is a famous name in which sport?
    - ⊔ Football
    - ⊔ Tennis
    - ⊔ Rugby Union

ANSWERS ON P.277

13. Valderrama, the venue of the 1997 Ryder Cup, is a golf course in which country?
    ⌐ Spain
    ⌐ Italy
    ⌐ France

14. What is the term for a short punch in boxing made with the elbow bent and rigid?
    ⌐ Clinch
    ⌐ Weave
    ⌐ Hook

15. Charlton Athletic Football Club is based in which English city?
    ⌐ Birmingham
    ⌐ London
    ⌐ Manchester

16. Mike Coughlan and Nigel Stepney made the news in 2007 by being involved in allegations of espionage in which sport?
    ⌐ Boxing
    ⌐ Formula 1
    ⌐ Rugby Union

17. Where was the snooker player Ray Reardon born?
    ⌐ Northern Ireland
    ⌐ Scotland
    ⌐ Wales

18. Which non-contact sport, first introduced by Sam Jacks in 1963 in Ontario, is sometimes described as 'floor hockey on ice'?
    ⌐ Ringette
    ⌐ Stoolball
    ⌐ Buzkashi

ANSWERS ON P.277

19. What name is given to the act of one or both boxers holding the other in order to hinder punches?
- ⊔ Grapple
- ⊔ Squeeze
- ⊔ Clinch

20. In terms of horse-racing, for what do the letters 'S.P.' stand?
- ⊔ Starting Price
- ⊔ Starting Penalty
- ⊔ Starting Position

21. 'Like riding a bicycle around your living room' was how Nelson Piquet decribed racing on which Formula 1 track?
- ⊔ Silverstone
- ⊔ Monza
- ⊔ Monaco

22. Which English county cricket team plays its home matches at the Rose Bowl?
- ⊔ Surrey
- ⊔ Hampshire
- ⊔ Leicestershire

23. Which footballer scored the penalty that took Ireland to their first ever World Cup quarter final in 1990?
- ⊔ Ray Houghton
- ⊔ John Aldridge
- ⊔ David O'Leary

24. Which England rugby union player's autobiography is entitled *Landing on My Feet*?
- ⊔ Mike Catt
- ⊔ Lawrence Dallaglio
- ⊔ Richard Hill

ANSWERS ON P.277

25. The term 'Tifosi' is applied to followers of which Formula 1 team?
   ⊔ McLaren
   ⊔ Ferrari
   ⊔ Honda

26. In netball, the only attacking players who are allowed in the goal circle are the goal shooter and which other?
   ⊔ Goal Tender
   ⊔ Goal Winger
   ⊔ Goal Attack

27. In the Olympics, how many players are there on each team in a game of beach-volleyball?
   ⊔ Four
   ⊔ Three
   ⊔ Two

28. Which British middleweight boxer is nicknamed the 'Battersea Bomber'?
   ⊔ Wayne Elcock
   ⊔ Bernard Hopkins
   ⊔ Howard Eastman

29. Kenny Dalglish scored 172 goals for which English football club?
   ⊔ Manchester United
   ⊔ Liverpool
   ⊔ Arsenal

30. What colour was the racehorse Desert Orchid?
   ⊔ Chestnut
   ⊔ Grey
   ⊔ Bay

ANSWERS ON P.277

31. The fast bowler Allan Donald represented which country in international cricket?
- ⌐ South Africa
- ⌐ Australia
- ⌐ West Indies

32. In the 1980s, Yuri Zakharevich was crowned both junior *and* the senior world champion in which sport?
- ⌐ Gymnastics
- ⌐ Weightlifting
- ⌐ Swimming

33. What nationality is the champion motorcyclist Valentino Rossi?
- ⌐ French
- ⌐ Italian
- ⌐ Spanish

34. 'Trebles for show, doubles for dough' is an old saying in which popular sport?
- ⌐ Snooker
- ⌐ Golf
- ⌐ Darts

35. In which sport did the Austrian Franz Klammer win an Olympic gold medal in 1976?
- ⌐ Skiing
- ⌐ Athletics
- ⌐ Rowing

36. In which year was the Ryder Cup golf tournament first played?
- ⌐ 1927
- ⌐ 1827
- ⌐ 1727

ANSWERS ON P.277

37. What name is given to an easy catch in cricket?
   ⌴ Daisy
   ⌴ Dotty
   ⌴ Dolly

38. For which international football team does Yossi Benayoun play?
   ⌴ Russia
   ⌴ Morocco
   ⌴ Israel

39. What natural material, obtained from the intestines of animals, has been used for the strings of tennis rackets?
   ⌴ Ambergris
   ⌴ Catgut
   ⌴ Shellac

40. To the nearest £100m, what was the total cost of the New Wembley Stadium?
   ⌴ £400m
   ⌴ £600m
   ⌴ £800m

41. The martial art of savate, literally meaning 'old shoe', originated in which country?
   ⌴ Egypt
   ⌴ France
   ⌴ Israel

42. What is the name of the shot in tennis where a player returns the ball to his opponent before it has a chance to bounce?
   ⌴ Boast
   ⌴ Volley
   ⌴ Parry

ANSWERS ON P.277

43. Who won the 1972 BBC Sports Personality of the Year Award?
⌴ Mary Peters
⌴ Virginia Wade
⌴ Tessa Sanderson

44. The Hahnenkamm is an annual race in which sport?
⌴ Skiing
⌴ Motor Racing
⌴ Cycling

45. At St Andrews Golf Course, Hell Bunker is a feature of which hole?
⌴ 4th
⌴ 7th
⌴ 14th

46. Simon Shaw and Josh Lewsey have represented England in which sport?
⌴ Cricket
⌴ Rugby Union
⌴ Football

47. The TV presenter Annabel Croft is a former British number one in which sport?
⌴ Show Jumping
⌴ Tennis
⌴ Athletics

48. What colour is the belt worn by a novice at judo?
⌴ White
⌴ Blue
⌴ Yellow

ANSWERS ON P.277

49. 'I'm Forever Blowing Bubbles' is a song traditionally associated with the supporters of which football club?
  ⊔ Leeds United
  ⊔ West Ham United
  ⊔ Manchester United

50. The Whitaker brothers, John and Michael, are world famous names in which sport?
  ⊔ Show Jumping
  ⊔ Skiing
  ⊔ Polo

51. In which former country was the 2004 Wimbledon tennis champion Maria Sharapova born?
  ⊔ Yugoslavia
  ⊔ Soviet Union
  ⊔ Czechoslovakia

52. In 1997, David Graveney became the chairman of selectors for the England team in which sport?
  ⊔ Cricket
  ⊔ Rugby Union
  ⊔ Hockey

53. The boxer Barry McGuigan was a world champion in which weight division in the 1980s?
  ⊔ Middleweight
  ⊔ Featherweight
  ⊔ Welterweight

54. The Owls is the nickname of which Yorkshire-based football team?
  ⊔ Sheffield Wednesday
  ⊔ Leeds United
  ⊔ Bradford City

ANSWERS ON P.277

55. What is the shortest sprint race contested at the World Indoor Athletic Championships?
 ⌐⌐ 50 Metres
 ⌐⌐ 60 Metres
 ⌐⌐ 80 Metres

56. Traditionally, the core of a cricket ball is made from which material?
 ⌐⌐ Willow
 ⌐⌐ Clay
 ⌐⌐ Cork

57. Which Rugby Union trophy is contested between Australia and New Zealand?
 ⌐⌐ The Meads/Eales Cup
 ⌐⌐ The James Bevan Trophy
 ⌐⌐ The Bledisloe Cup

58. Continental, eastern and semi-western are types of grip used in which sport?
 ⌐⌐ Tennis
 ⌐⌐ Fencing
 ⌐⌐ Golf

59. Which golfer has been runner-up at the Open Championship a record seven times?
 ⌐⌐ Gary Player
 ⌐⌐ Jack Nicklaus
 ⌐⌐ Greg Norman

60. The Emirates Stadium became the home ground of which London football team in July 2006?
 ⌐⌐ Tottenham Hotspur
 ⌐⌐ Millwall
 ⌐⌐ Arsenal

ANSWERS ON P.277

61. By what name is a boxer's assistant traditionally known?
    ⊔ First
    ⊔ Second
    ⊔ Third

62. In which Olympic sport are competitors commonly referred to as 'sliders'?
    ⊔ Snowboarding
    ⊔ Ice Dancing
    ⊔ Luge

63. According to World Snooker, what is the minimum permissible length for a cue in professional competition?
    ⊔ 3 Feet
    ⊔ 4 Feet
    ⊔ 5 Feet

64. Which football team play their home matches at Pride Park Stadium?
    ⊔ Derby County
    ⊔ Middlesbrough
    ⊔ Wigan Athletic

65. Torpids and Eights Week are events in which sport?
    ⊔ Rowing
    ⊔ Skiing
    ⊔ Boxing

66. Which Indian cricketer was known as 'The Haryana Hurricane'?
    ⊔ Kapil Dev
    ⊔ Sunil Gavaskar
    ⊔ Bishen Bedi

ANSWERS ON P.277

67. For which international cricket team did Brian Lara play?
- New Zealand
- Zimbabwe
- West Indies

68. Who scored four tries for New Zealand against England in the semi-final of the 1995 Rugby Union World Cup?
- Christian Cullen
- Doug Howlett
- Jonah Lomu

69. What is the distance of the swimming section of an Olympic Triathlon?
- 500m
- 1500m
- 5000m

70. 'Hitch-kick', 'sail' and 'hang' are all techniques used by competitors in which athletics event?
- 100m
- Long Jump
- Pole Vault

71. The basketball player Kareem Abdul-Jabbar won five NBA titles in the 1980s playing for which team?
- LA Lakers
- Utah Jazz
- Boston Celtics

72. How many feet long is a competition standard table tennis table?
- 9
- 12
- 15

ANSWERS ON P.277

73. How many points is a 'double top' worth in a game of darts?
⌐ Ten
⌐ Forty
⌐ Sixty

74. Which English city is the home of Aston Villa football club?
⌐ Birmingham
⌐ London
⌐ Manchester

75. Thomas Bjorn of Denmark is a leading competitor in which sport?
⌐ Badminton
⌐ Golf
⌐ Cycling

76. The Formula 1 Grand Prix of which country is raced at the Spa-Francorchamps circuit?
⌐ Italy
⌐ Argentina
⌐ Belgium

77. What is the diameter of a table tennis ball according to Olympic regulations?
⌐ 40mm
⌐ 70mm
⌐ 90mm

78. In 1959, which British tennis player became the youngest person to win the Ladies' Singles title at the French Open?
⌐ Virginia Wade
⌐ Christine Truman
⌐ Angela Mortimer

ANSWERS ON P.277

79. 'Shakehands' is the name of the prevalent grip used in which sport?
- ⌴ Table Tennis
- ⌴ Badminton
- ⌴ Darts

80. Which country won the Football World Cup in 1978 and 1986?
- ⌴ Argentina
- ⌴ Italy
- ⌴ Mexico

81. Fergal O'Brien is a famous name in which sport?
- ⌴ Cricket
- ⌴ Snooker
- ⌴ Motorcycling

82. What is the width between the goal posts in a standard outdoor polo match?
- ⌴ 4 Yards
- ⌴ 8 Yards
- ⌴ 16 Yards

83. What name is given to the snooker rest with widely arched legs which offers several cueing positions?
- ⌴ Jaws
- ⌴ Spider
- ⌴ Cannon

84. Bill Edrich and his younger cousin John Edrich both represented England at which sport in the 20th century?
- ⌴ Rugby Union
- ⌴ Cricket
- ⌴ Football

ANSWERS ON P.277

85. Which member of the Royal family became President of the Football Association in May 2006?
- ⬜ Prince William
- ⬜ Prince Harry
- ⬜ Prince Charles

86. In which sport at the 1976 Olympic Games did East German Kornelia Ender win four gold medals?
- ⬜ Athletics
- ⬜ Gymnastics
- ⬜ Swimming

87. 'Chip and run', 'back nine' and 'out of bounds' are terms commonly used in which sport?
- ⬜ Golf
- ⬜ Snooker
- ⬜ Tennis

88. Which football manager dubbed himself the 'Special One' on his arrival in England in 2004?
- ⬜ Arsene Wenger
- ⬜ José Mourinho
- ⬜ Rafael Benitez

89. Andy Ripley represented England in the 1970s in which sport?
- ⬜ Football
- ⬜ Athletics
- ⬜ Rugby Union

90. In which country is the test match cricket venue of Galle?
- ⬜ Sri Lanka
- ⬜ South Africa
- ⬜ Pakistan

ANSWERS ON P.277

91. Which British driver has won the most Formula 1 World Championships?
- ⏜ Jackie Stewart
- ⏜ James Hunt
- ⏜ Nigel Mansell

92. Which businessman started World Series Cricket in 1977 introducing, amongst other things, coloured kit into the game?
- ⏜ Rupert Murdoch
- ⏜ Alan Sugar
- ⏜ Kerry Packer

93. In a game of 8-ball pool, what name is given to the balls of a solid colour, numbered between 1 and 7?
- ⏜ Spots
- ⏜ Stars
- ⏜ Slams

94. Rebound tumbling is an alternative name for which sport?
- ⏜ Judo
- ⏜ Synchronised Swimming
- ⏜ Trampolining

95. Brian Gamlin is credited with making a major contribution to the appearance of which game in the 19th century?
- ⏜ Bowls
- ⏜ Croquet
- ⏜ Darts

96. Which was the last Summer Olympics at which Great Britain came top of the medal table?
- ⏜ Athens 1896
- ⏜ London 1908
- ⏜ London 1948

ANSWERS ON P.277

97. Giuseppe Farina won the first Formula 1 World Championship in 1950 driving which make of car?
- ⌷ McLaren
- ⌷ Alfa Romeo
- ⌷ Honda

98. In Olympic-style amateur boxing, what is the heaviest weight division?
- ⌷ Super Heavyweight
- ⌷ Heavyweight
- ⌷ Light Heavyweight

99. Phillips Idowu represents Great Britain at which athletics event?
- ⌷ Long Jump
- ⌷ High Jump
- ⌷ Triple Jump

100. The martial art tae kwon do originated in which country?
- ⌷ Japan
- ⌷ Korea
- ⌷ Thailand

ANSWERS ON P.277

1. Which monarch awarded Sir Francis Drake his knighthood?
   ⊔ Henry VIII
   ⊔ Mary I
   ⊔ Elizabeth I

2. In the 1820s, Constable painted a view of which structure from 'the Bishop's Ground'?
   ⊔ Balliol College
   ⊔ Westminster Bridge
   ⊔ Salisbury Cathedral

3. What is the name of Ophelia's brother in the Shakespeare play *Hamlet*?
   ⊔ Claudius
   ⊔ Polonius
   ⊔ Laertes

4. Christian is a middle name of which child of Prince Philip and Queen Elizabeth II?
   ⊔ Prince Edward
   ⊔ Prince Andrew
   ⊔ Prince Charles

5. In which year were Uri Geller, André the Giant and Carl XVI Gustaf of Sweden born?
   ⊔ 1946
   ⊔ 1951
   ⊔ 1956

6. What type of garments are 'reefers' and 'bombers'?
   ⊔ Skirts
   ⊔ Jackets
   ⊔ Ties

ANSWERS ON P.278

7. Lindow Man, popularly known as Pete Marsh, is the preserved body of an early man, usually kept on display in which museum?
   - ⌴ Natural History Museum
   - ⌴ Science Museum
   - ⌴ British Museum

8. Odo, Bishop of Bayeux, who became Earl of Kent, was the half-brother of which king?
   - ⌴ Edward I
   - ⌴ Richard I
   - ⌴ William I

9. 'Alouette' is the French name for which bird?
   - ⌴ Nightingale
   - ⌴ Sparrow
   - ⌴ Lark

10. Which psychoanalytical concept is also known as 'parapraxis'?
   - ⌴ Freudian Slip
   - ⌴ Primal Scream
   - ⌴ Collective Consciousness

11. The architect Otto Wagner designed many Art Nouveau-style stations for a rail system of which city?
   - ⌴ Vienna
   - ⌴ Berlin
   - ⌴ Prague

12. Woodford, in Essex, was the last constituency held by which Prime Minister?
   - ⌴ Stanley Baldwin
   - ⌴ Winston Churchill
   - ⌴ David Lloyd-George

ANSWERS ON P.278

13. The approximately 300-square-mile plateau known as Salisbury Plain is in which English county?
    ⊔ Northumberland
    ⊔ Cheshire
    ⊔ Wiltshire

14. 'Pobol y Cym', the longest-running BBC TV soap, is based in which part of the UK?
    ⊔ Northern Ireland
    ⊔ Wales
    ⊔ Scotland

15. Which singer, who had a UK number one single in the 1960s, married the songwriter Tony Hatch in 1967?
    ⊔ Jackie Trent
    ⊔ Judith Durham
    ⊔ Jane Birkin

16. What term is used to refer to an organised body of hired applauders in the theatre?
    ⊔ Clique
    ⊔ Claque
    ⊔ Cloque

17. In the 19th century, Hippolyte Bayard was a pioneer of which technology?
    ⊔ Photography
    ⊔ Vaccination
    ⊔ Heavier-than-air Flight

18. Johann Zoffany became famous in England during the 18th century in which profession?
    ⊔ Landscape Gardener
    ⊔ Composer
    ⊔ Painter

ANSWERS ON P.278

19. Which American writer is best known for his 1930s novel
Anthony Adverse?
- ⌣ Oliver La Farge
- ⌣ Hervey Allen
- ⌣ John Phillips Marquand

20. Which medieval monastery was located in the Vale of the
Deadly Nightshade?
- ⌣ Beaulieu Abbey
- ⌣ Meaux Abbey
- ⌣ Furness Abbey

21. The book *Beyond the Crash*, published in 2010, was written
by which former Prime Minister?
- ⌣ John Major
- ⌣ Tony Blair
- ⌣ Gordon Brown

22. Which pop star made headlines in 2010 when she wore a
dress purportedly made out of raw meat?
- ⌣ Lady Gaga
- ⌣ Rihanna
- ⌣ Cheryl Cole

23. Filton Airport serves which English city?
- ⌣ Plymouth
- ⌣ Bristol
- ⌣ Exeter

24. Who is most likely to use a Snellen chart in their place of
work?
- ⌣ Podiatrist
- ⌣ Chiropractor
- ⌣ Optometrist

ANSWERS ON P.278

25. George Raynor managed which football team to the final of the 1958 World Cup?
- ⊔ Uruguay
- ⊔ Italy
- ⊔ Sweden

26. Which American entertainer was UNICEF's first Goodwill Ambassador, appointed in 1954?
- ⊔ Danny Kaye
- ⊔ Lucille Ball
- ⊔ Bob Hope

27. The region once known as Bactria is on which continent?
- ⊔ Asia
- ⊔ South America
- ⊔ Africa

28. What is the chief setting for the 1930s British film comedy *Oh, Mr Porter!*?
- ⊔ Hotel
- ⊔ Hospital
- ⊔ Railway Station

29. The CSP is the professional body and trade union for which professionals in the UK?
- ⊔ Physiotherapists
- ⊔ Paediatricians
- ⊔ Plumbers

30. For which invention did Peter Durand receive a patent in 1810?
- ⊔ Sliced Bread
- ⊔ Zip Fastener
- ⊔ Tin Can

ANSWERS ON P.278

31. In which year was Prince Andrew, the Duke of York, born?
- ⌴ 1957
- ⌴ 1960
- ⌴ 1963

32. How many dominoes are there in a standard, or double-six, set?
- ⌴ 20
- ⌴ 24
- ⌴ 28

33. What is the meaning of the word 'mordacious'?
- ⌴ Sarcastic
- ⌴ Humble
- ⌴ Untruthful

34. In which country does the action in Bizet's opera *The Pearl Fishers* take place?
- ⌴ Persia
- ⌴ Ceylon
- ⌴ Siam

35. In the standard notation for the card game bridge, for what does the abbreviation 'NT' stand?
- ⌴ Next Turn
- ⌴ No Trumps
- ⌴ New Trick

36. What type of creature is the cartoon character Foghorn Leghorn?
- ⌴ Alligator
- ⌴ Rooster
- ⌴ Hare

ANSWERS ON P.278

37. How many dots are there in the Morse code for 'SOS'?
   ⌴ 4
   ⌴ 6
   ⌴ 8

38. Camelopard is an archaic name for which creature?
   ⌴ Elephant
   ⌴ Zebra
   ⌴ Giraffe

39. How many Grand Prix races did David Coulthard win during his Formula 1 career?
   ⌴ 13
   ⌴ 28
   ⌴ 43

40. What is the term for the worship of one god while conceding that other gods exist too?
   ⌴ Henotheism
   ⌴ Panentheism
   ⌴ Hypotheism

41. In 2011, who took over from Nancy Pelosi as Speaker of the US House of Representatives?
   ⌴ John Boehner
   ⌴ Tom Price
   ⌴ Pete Sessions

42. In which year were the businessman Richard Branson, the singer Karen Carpenter and the TV presenter Jay Leno born?
   ⌴ 1945
   ⌴ 1950
   ⌴ 1955

ANSWERS ON P.278

43. For what does the letter 'J' stand in the name of the author
J.M. Barrie?
- ⊔ James
- ⊔ Jeremy
- ⊔ John

44. Who did Mehmet Ali Ağca shoot in May 1981?
- ⊔ John Lennon
- ⊔ Ronald Reagan
- ⊔ Pope John Paul II

45. 'Start Without You' was a UK number one single in 2010 for
which former *X Factor* contestant?
- ⊔ Alexandra Burke
- ⊔ Olly Murs
- ⊔ Diana Vickers

46. What is the main ingredient of the French soup 'billi bi'?
- ⊔ Crab
- ⊔ Oysters
- ⊔ Mussels

47. In motoring, for what does the letter 'S' stand in the
government agency abbreviation DSA?
- ⊔ Standards
- ⊔ School
- ⊔ Signs

48. Which singer and actress married Marc Anthony in 2004?
- ⊔ Jennifer Lopez
- ⊔ Madonna
- ⊔ Beyoncé

ANSWERS ON P.278

49. The TV comedy *30 Rock* is named after the address of the headquarters of which American television network?
  ⊔ ABC
  ⊔ NBC
  ⊔ CBS

50. What type of garment is the 'guayabera' which was made an official formal dress garment in Cuba in 2010?
  ⊔ Shirt
  ⊔ Jacket
  ⊔ Waistcoat

51. Cerussite is a carbonate of which metal?
  ⊔ Lead
  ⊔ Manganese
  ⊔ Potassium

52. Which secretion is produced by the sublingual and submandibular glands?
  ⊔ Adrenalin
  ⊔ Tears
  ⊔ Saliva

53. What is encased in pastry in the Scottish delicacy called a black bun?
  ⊔ Fruit Cake
  ⊔ Chocolate Cake
  ⊔ Coffee Cake

54. The nickname 'Mr Cricket' became synonymous with which Australian cricketer?
  ⊔ Shane Watson
  ⊔ Mike Hussey
  ⊔ Brad Haddin

ANSWERS ON P.278

55. What was the surname of Samantha Cameron before her marriage to the politician David Cameron?
    ⊔ Leeds
    ⊔ Sheffield
    ⊔ Bradford

56. Which actor has appeared in the films *Déjà Vu*, *Inside Man* and *The Bone Collector*?
    ⊔ Will Smith
    ⊔ Denzel Washington
    ⊔ Eddie Murphy

57. Mam Tor in Derbyshire is known as the 'Shivering . . .' what?
    ⊔ Lake
    ⊔ Mountain
    ⊔ Forest

58. Invercargill is a city in which country?
    ⊔ South Africa
    ⊔ New Zealand
    ⊔ Canada

59. What is the title of the 2010 sequel to Scott Turow's 1987 novel *Presumed Innocent*?
    ⊔ The Confession
    ⊔ Presumed Guilty
    ⊔ Innocent

60. The expression 'it was Greek to me' is a quotation from which of Shakespeare's plays?
    ⊔ Timon of Athens
    ⊔ Antony and Cleopatra
    ⊔ Julius Caesar

ANSWERS ON P.278

61. Who was the UK's Foreign Secretary during the Suez Crisis?
- Herbert Morrison
- Alec Douglas-Home
- Selwyn Lloyd

62. What flower is traditionally used as an emblem of England?
- Daisy
- Rose
- Violet

63. What name is given to the casing in which vanilla seeds are housed?
- Pouch
- Purse
- Pod

64. The 1954 football World Cup, which was won by West Germany, was held in which European country?
- Italy
- Netherlands
- Switzerland

65. To which order of reptiles do snakes and lizards belong?
- Squamata
- Testudines
- Crocodilia

66. Which member of the Rolling Stones released the 2010 autobiography entitled *Life*?
- Ronnie Wood
- Keith Richards
- Mick Jagger

ANSWERS ON P.278

67. Benigno Aquino became president of which country in 2010?
- ⊔ Indonesia
- ⊔ Vietnam
- ⊔ Philippines

68. What nickname is given to the book used by trainee London taxi drivers which acts as a guide to learning the knowledge?
- ⊔ Blue Book
- ⊔ Red Book
- ⊔ Yellow Book

69. The fashion designer Jeff Banks married which singer in the 1960s?
- ⊔ Lulu
- ⊔ Sandie Shaw
- ⊔ Marianne Faithfull

70. Which poet described Oxford as 'that sweet city with her dreaming spires' in his poem 'Thyrsis'?
- ⊔ Matthew Arnold
- ⊔ John Betjeman
- ⊔ William Blake

71. In the 1942 Disney cartoon *Donald Gets Drafted*, what was revealed to be the middle name of Donald Duck?
- ⊔ Pimpernel
- ⊔ Fauntleroy
- ⊔ Moriarty

72. Which fruit is referred to in French as 'pamplemousse'?
- ⊔ Lemon
- ⊔ Grapefruit
- ⊔ Banana

ANSWERS ON P.278

73. Which term was used to refer to the act of levelling a fortification or castle to the ground?
- ⌣ Slim
- ⌣ Slender
- ⌣ Slight

74. What name is given to a joint of beef consisting of two sirloins left uncut at the backbone?
- ⌣ Baron
- ⌣ Duke
- ⌣ Lord

75. Tsar Alexis Mikhailovich, who died in 1676, was the father of which historical figure?
- ⌣ Ivan the Terrible
- ⌣ Peter the Great
- ⌣ Genghis Khan

76. A statue by Joseph Boehm of which scientist is prominently displayed at the Natural History Museum?
- ⌣ Robert Boyle
- ⌣ Charles Darwin
- ⌣ William Herschel

77. Which actor, a BAFTA Rising Star Award winner, directed the films *Adulthood* and *4.3.2.1*?
- ⌣ Matt Smith
- ⌣ Noel Clarke
- ⌣ John Simm

78. One of Peter Mandelson's first jobs was as a producer on which television programme?
- ⌣ Panorama
- ⌣ Newsnight
- ⌣ Weekend World

ANSWERS ON P.278

79. 'Tawny' is a type of which drink?
   ⊔ Whisky
   ⊔ Port
   ⊔ Brandy

80. Telugu is a language primarily spoken in which country?
   ⊔ India
   ⊔ Australia
   ⊔ Morocco

81. Who became the first emperor of a united Germany in
   1871?
   ⊔ Karl I
   ⊔ Wilhelm I
   ⊔ Heinrich I

82. Llaima is an active volcano in which country?
   ⊔ Chile
   ⊔ Argentina
   ⊔ Ecuador

83. In Arthurian legend, which knight is usually said to have
   returned Excalibur to the Lady of the Lake?
   ⊔ Pelleas
   ⊔ Lamorak
   ⊔ Bedivere

84. José Mourinho worked as an assistant and interpreter for
   which English football manager in Spain and Portugal in the
   1990s?
   ⊔ Bobby Robson
   ⊔ Malcolm Allison
   ⊔ Harry Redknapp

ANSWERS ON P.278

85. Who wrote the children's classic *The Owl Service*, basing it on traditional Welsh legends?
   - Alan Garner
   - Philippa Pearce
   - Terry Pratchett

86. Which novel by Ben Elton was adapted by him into a play which won the 1998 Laurence Olivier Award for Best New Comedy?
   - Dead Famous
   - Stark
   - Popcorn

87. Who became president of the Woodland Trust in 2004?
   - Jeremy Clarkson
   - Graham Norton
   - Clive Anderson

88. Which vegetable is the principal ingredient of Saxe-Coburg soup?
   - Carrot
   - Brussels Sprout
   - Parsnip

89. In which US state did John Harvey Kellogg run the famous Battle Creek Sanitarium, a centre for dietary reform?
   - Michigan
   - Maine
   - Massachusetts

90. In which 20th-century war did UK troops take part in the Battle of the Imjin River?
   - World War II
   - Spanish Civil War
   - Korean War

ANSWERS ON P.278

91. In which European country did women receive the right to vote in 1971?
- ⊔ France
- ⊔ Germany
- ⊔ Switzerland

92. Which UK Eurovision Song Contest-winning group was fronted by an American?
- ⊔ Bucks Fizz
- ⊔ Brotherhood of Man
- ⊔ Katrina and the Waves

93. What is the literal translation of 'Dies Irae', the name of part of the Roman Catholic Requiem Mass?
- ⊔ He Is Dead
- ⊔ Perpetual Light
- ⊔ Day of Wrath

94. The Australian kelpie is a breed of which domestic creature?
- ⊔ Dog
- ⊔ Cat
- ⊔ Rabbit

95. In 2010, Thierry Henry left Barcelona to join which Major League soccer team?
- ⊔ Chicago Fire
- ⊔ New York Red Bulls
- ⊔ Houston Dynamo

96. Norrin Radd is the alter ego of which comic book superhero?
- ⊔ Doctor Strange
- ⊔ Silver Surfer
- ⊔ Daredevil

ANSWERS ON P.278

97. Which Nobel Prize-winning playwright died in 1950 at the age of ninety-four?
  ⊔ Noël Coward
  ⊔ Terence Rattigan
  ⊔ George Bernard Shaw

98. Who is the subject of the Michael Crick book subtitled *Stranger Than Fiction*?
  ⊔ David Beckham
  ⊔ Jeffrey Archer
  ⊔ Michael Jackson

99. Which canton of Switzerland was only created in 1979 when it was separated from the canton of Bern?
  ⊔ Valais
  ⊔ Jura
  ⊔ Uri

100. In which decade was the *Radio Times* first published?
  ⊔ 1920s
  ⊔ 1930s
  ⊔ 1940s

ANSWERS ON P.278

BARRY SIMMONS

FULL NAME:
Barry Lawrence Simmons

HOME TOWN:
Edinburgh, but I live in Leeds

EDUCATION:
BSc (Spec Hons) Chemistry
C Dip A&F (Certified Diploma in Accountancy and Finance)
Diploma in Systems Analysis

QUIZZING CREDENTIALS:

Winner *Brain of Britain*	2013
Winner *Are You an Egghead?*	2008
Finalist *Brain of Britain*	2008
Radio 4 *Masterteam* Champion	2007
Semi-finalist *Mastermind*	2005
Who Wants to Be a Millionaire	2005, winning £64,000
Runner-up *European Quizzing*	2005
Championships (Team England)	

Come and Have a Go If You Think You're 2004, shared winnings
   Smart Enough   of £40,000
Won *European Quizzing Championships* 2004
   (Team England)
6 Five Towns Quiz League & Cup double
2 Airedale Quiz League championships
Winner of 6 West Yorkshire Airebrains
Current member Scotland Quiz Team

LEAST FAVOURITE SUBJECT:
I like and enjoy all subjects.

SPECIAL INTEREST:
Astronomy has a special place in my heart as it is such a fascinating subject.

HOBBIES:
I am an enthusiastic amateur Graphologist with over fifteen years experience, so watch out if I see your handwriting as I can identify the hidden secrets of your character. I also enjoy playing the Japanese game of Go.

WHAT DOES IT TAKE TO BE AN EGGHEAD:
Intense curiosity over a very wide range of subjects, good memory and excellent recall.

WHO WOULD BE ON YOUR ULTIMATE FANTASY QUIZ TEAM:
Quizzing should be fun as well as informative, so my ultimate team would include Stephen Fry, Billy Connolly and Victoria Coren. Nobody would notice if we got an answer wrong because they would be laughing so much!

MOST MEMORABLE MOMENT DURING YOUR TIME AS AN EGGHEAD:
The first time I took on a team of five players on my own and won. I was given a magnum of champagne to celebrate by our producer. The second time it happened I got nothing as I was told 'Well we know you can do it now!'

WHAT ADVICE DO YOU HAVE FOR ANY BUDDING EGGHEADS:

Read, read, and then read some more, but avoid learning lists. They are so boring! As a minimum you must read a quality newspaper from cover to cover each day.

WHAT IS YOUR FAVOURITE FACT/ PIECE OF TRIVIA:

Which father and daughter are represented by elements in the Periodic Table? Answer Tantalus and Niobe (Tantalum and Niobium). I love this question as it requires deep knowledge of two different fields, Science and Greek mythology, both of which are favourite interests of mine.

LITTLE KNOWN FACT ABOUT YOU:

In 1980 I danced on the stage of Caesar's Palace in Las Vegas with Diana Ross.

1. The two most abundant elements that compose the Sun are helium and which other?
   ␣ Hydrogen
   ␣ Carbon
   ␣ Argon

2. Which branch of medicine deals with diseases and conditions specific to the male sex?
   ␣ Nephrology
   ␣ Pulmonology
   ␣ Andrology

3. What is the name of the endangered wildcat that is native to Spain?
   ␣ Iberian Cougar
   ␣ Iberian Lynx
   ␣ Iberian Ocelot

4. Who discovered and lent his name to the citric acid cycle that is central to the metabolism of virtually all living organisms?
   ␣ Hans Krebs
   ␣ Aaron Klug
   ␣ Harry Kroto

5. Which part of the United States has reported a major ecological problem due to the presence of thousands of Burmese pythons?
   ␣ Badlands National Park
   ␣ Catskill Mountains
   ␣ Florida Everglades

6. How many atoms are there in a molecule of water?
   ␣ 2
   ␣ 3
   ␣ 5

ANSWERS ON P.279

7. Which branch of mathematics takes its name from the Greek for 'to measure land'?
   ⊔ Statistics
   ⊔ Calculus
   ⊔ Geometry

8. The condition 'seborrhoea' primarily affects which organ of the body?
   ⊔ Brain
   ⊔ Liver
   ⊔ Skin

9. What type of creature is a corncrake?
   ⊔ Spider
   ⊔ Bird
   ⊔ Rodent

10. What is the chemical symbol for the element radon?
    ⊔ Rn
    ⊔ Rh
    ⊔ Ra

11. In which year did the International Space Station receive its first crew?
    ⊔ 1995
    ⊔ 2000
    ⊔ 2005

12. Approximately how many Earth years does it take the planet Neptune to orbit the sun?
    ⊔ 85 years
    ⊔ 125 years
    ⊔ 165 years

ANSWERS ON P.279

13. The glyptodon was an early relation of which mammal?
    ⊔ Platypus
    ⊔ Armadillo
    ⊔ Giraffe

14. Cycling's three Grand Tours are those of France, Spain and
    which other country?
    ⊔ Italy
    ⊔ Germany
    ⊔ Russia

15. How many legs does an ant have?
    ⊔ 6
    ⊔ 8
    ⊔ 10

16. What is the name of the group of galaxies to which the Milky
    Way belongs?
    ⊔ District Group
    ⊔ Local Group
    ⊔ Neighbourhood Group

17. Which metal was historically produced by a technique
    known as 'puddling'?
    ⊔ Iron
    ⊔ Zinc
    ⊔ Silver

18. What type of drug is streptomycin?
    ⊔ Anti-inflammatory
    ⊔ Antibiotic
    ⊔ Antihistamine

ANSWERS ON P.279

19. Which parts of the body may be affected by pyelitis?
  ⊔ Lungs
  ⊔ Eyes
  ⊔ Kidneys

20. What type of creature is the Australian 'thorny devil'?
  ⊔ Spider
  ⊔ Lizard
  ⊔ Shark

21. Which constellation represents a swan?
  ⊔ Apus
  ⊔ Pavo
  ⊔ Cygnus

22. What would be studied by an odontologist?
  ⊔ Eggs
  ⊔ Mountains
  ⊔ Teeth

23. What is the name of the monkey species discovered in 2010, which is said to sneeze when it rains?
  ⊔ Myanmar Snub-Nosed
  ⊔ Laos Flat-Nosed
  ⊔ Thai Red-Nosed

24. Which mineral is listed at number 9 on the Mohs' scale, one below diamond?
  ⊔ Corundum
  ⊔ Topaz
  ⊔ Quartz

ANSWERS ON P.279

25. The Silurian period occurred in which geological era?
  ⊔ Palaeozoic
  ⊔ Mesozoic
  ⊔ Cenozoic

26. What term is used to refer to low-volume electrical or radio noise of equal intensity over a wide range of frequencies?
  ⊔ Indigo Noise
  ⊔ White Noise
  ⊔ Yellow Noise

27. What type of bird of prey is a hobby?
  ⊔ Owl
  ⊔ Vulture
  ⊔ Falcon

28. The prehistoric creatures called 'trilobites', that are often found as fossils, lived in which environment?
  ⊔ Desert
  ⊔ Rainforest
  ⊔ Sea

29. What was the code name of the first atomic bomb test that was carried out in New Mexico in July 1945?
  ⊔ Triad
  ⊔ Trinity
  ⊔ Troika

30. What term is given to any disease that can be passed from non-human animals to humans?
  ⊔ Zoonosis
  ⊔ Phage
  ⊔ Virion

ANSWERS ON P.279

31. Where is the Gutenberg Discontinuity?
- ⌊⌋ Between Uranus and Neptune
- ⌊⌋ Inside the Brain
- ⌊⌋ Within the Earth

32. Which 19th-century scientist is credited with the invention of the pilot, or cow-catcher, on the front of railway locomotives?
- ⌊⌋ Charles Darwin
- ⌊⌋ Charles Lyell
- ⌊⌋ Charles Babbage

33. How did German chemist J. Wilbrand intend TNT to be used when he discovered it in 1863?
- ⌊⌋ Glue
- ⌊⌋ Flavour Enhancer
- ⌊⌋ Yellow Dye

34. What is the name of the projection at the tip of a young bird's beak which is used to break open the eggshell?
- ⌊⌋ Egg Leg
- ⌊⌋ Egg Tooth
- ⌊⌋ Egg Nail

35. The magnetron is a major component of which household appliance?
- ⌊⌋ Microwave Oven
- ⌊⌋ Vacuum Cleaner
- ⌊⌋ Television

36. What is the name of the rough skin of some sharks, used as an abrasive?
- ⌊⌋ Isinglass
- ⌊⌋ Shagreen
- ⌊⌋ Ambergris

ANSWERS ON P.279

37. What type of creature is the endangered Tana River mangabey?
   ⊔ Reptile
   ⊔ Primate
   ⊔ Bird

38. The superior rectus muscle is one of a set of muscles that control the movement of which part of the body?
   ⊔ Foot
   ⊔ Shoulder
   ⊔ Eyeball

39. What term is used to refer to an agent, such as a bacterium or virus, that can cause disease?
   ⊔ Histamine
   ⊔ Serotonin
   ⊔ Pathogen

40. The colourful species of kingfisher that is native to Britain has an orange-red breast and a back that is which other colour?
   ⊔ Yellow
   ⊔ Blue
   ⊔ Pink

41. Heron's formula refers to the area of which geometric shape?
   ⊔ Pentagon
   ⊔ Rectangle
   ⊔ Triangle

42. A dolorimeter is an instrument used to measure what?
   ⊔ Snowfall
   ⊔ Water Hardness
   ⊔ Pain

ANSWERS ON P.279

43. What is the chemical symbol of the element arsenic?
⊔ As
⊔ Ac
⊔ An

44. Which muscles enable some people to wiggle their ears?
⊔ Deltoid Muscles
⊔ Auricular Muscles
⊔ Intercostal Muscles

45. What nickname is given to the California headquarters of the internet company Google?
⊔ Googleplex
⊔ Googlelab
⊔ Googlebot

46. What type of creature is an 'indri'?
⊔ Wallaby
⊔ Toad
⊔ Lemur

47. The spice cinnamon is obtained from a tree that belongs to which family?
⊔ Beech
⊔ Laurel
⊔ Dogwood

48. Theta rhythms are waves generated in which part of the body?
⊔ Heart
⊔ Brain
⊔ Liver

ANSWERS ON P.279

49. In the Periodic Table, what is the atomic number of nitrogen?

⌐┘ 1
⌐┘ 4
⌐┘ 7

50. The American physicist Samuel T. Cohen, who died in 2010, was the inventor of which weapon?

⌐┘ Neutron Bomb
⌐┘ Cluster Bomb
⌐┘ Bouncing Bomb

51. The Zonule of Zinn is a ligament found in which part of the body?

⌐┘ Ear
⌐┘ Eye
⌐┘ Nose

52. Myrmecology is the scientific study of which creatures?

⌐┘ Ants
⌐┘ Spiders
⌐┘ Butterflies

53. In medicine, electrocardiography is primarily used to record the electrical activity of which part of the body?

⌐┘ Brain
⌐┘ Heart
⌐┘ Lungs

54. Which branch of scientific study is concerned with the uses and effects of drugs?

⌐┘ Physiology
⌐┘ Palaeontology
⌐┘ Pharmacology

ANSWERS ON P.279

55. James Prescott were the first names of which British scientist?
- ⊔ Gray
- ⊔ Joule
- ⊔ Kelvin

56. In chemistry, what is the SI unit for an amount of substance?
- ⊔ Mole
- ⊔ Weber
- ⊔ Siemens

57. What is the approximate melting point, in degrees Celsius, of pure gold?
- ⊔ 1,064
- ⊔ 2,064
- ⊔ 3,064

58. John Young and Charles Duke walked on the moon during which Apollo mission?
- ⊔ Apollo 9
- ⊔ Apollo 14
- ⊔ Apollo 16

59. A creature described as 'hispid' is covered in what?
- ⊔ Scales
- ⊔ Feathers
- ⊔ Bristles

60. What is the surface area, in centimetres squared, of a cube whose edges are 4cm in length?
- ⊔ 64
- ⊔ 80
- ⊔ 96

ANSWERS ON P.279

61. In what state does the chemical element barium exist at room temperature?
   ⊔ Solid
   ⊔ Liquid
   ⊔ Gas

62. In which part of the human body is the ischium found?
   ⊔ Knee
   ⊔ Hip
   ⊔ Shoulder

63. A neutron probe is a device normally used by geographers and farmers to detect the amount of what in soil?
   ⊔ Water
   ⊔ Nitrates
   ⊔ Calcium Carbonate

64. What name is given to the part of vision that detects objects outside the direct line of vision?
   ⊔ Perpendicular
   ⊔ Peripheral
   ⊔ Perfunctory

65. Smelting is a process used in the extraction of what?
   ⊔ Water
   ⊔ Oil
   ⊔ Metal

66. If something is described as being 'vitreous', what substance does it resemble?
   ⊔ Glass
   ⊔ Muscle
   ⊔ Wax

ANSWERS ON P.279

67. Which creatures belong to the order *Coleoptera*?
- ⌣ Beetles
- ⌣ Deer
- ⌣ Owls

68. Phylloquinone is another name for which vitamin?
- ⌣ Vitamin A1
- ⌣ Vitamin D1
- ⌣ Vitamin K1

69. The simple organism called an 'amoeba' is formed from how many cells?
- ⌣ 1
- ⌣ 100
- ⌣ 1,000

70. Spiders, scorpions and mites all belong to which class of creatures?
- ⌣ Amphibians
- ⌣ Arachnids
- ⌣ Annelids

71. Which fruit comes from the tree *Prunus armeniaca*?
- ⌣ Kiwi
- ⌣ Gooseberry
- ⌣ Apricot

72. In the standard layout of the Periodic Table, hydrogen and which other element are the only members of the first period?
- ⌣ Helium
- ⌣ Oxygen
- ⌣ Nitrogen

ANSWERS ON P.279

73. Who, at the age of forty-seven, is credited with being the oldest man to set foot on the moon?
- ☐ Buzz Aldrin
- ☐ John Young
- ☐ Alan Shepard

74. Which American evolutionary biologist wrote the popular science books *Ever Since Darwin* and *The Panda's Thumb*?
- ☐ Stephen Jay Gould
- ☐ E.O. Wilson
- ☐ Richard Lewontin

75. Gazelles are native to which parts of the world?
- ☐ Africa and Asia
- ☐ Australia and New Zealand
- ☐ North and South America

76. For what does the letter 'M' stand in the acronym 'CD-ROM'?
- ☐ Memory
- ☐ Music
- ☐ Microprocessor

77. In the human body, which substance is transported in the blood by high-density lipoprotein and low-density lipoprotein?
- ☐ Adrenaline
- ☐ Bone Marrow
- ☐ Cholesterol

78. What were the forenames of the German physicist Fahrenheit, who invented the mercury thermometer in 1714?
- ☐ Joshua Michael
- ☐ Daniel Gabriel
- ☐ Abraham Samuel

ANSWERS ON P.279

79. What does an autoclave use for sterilising surgical instruments?
- ⌣ Pressurised Steam
- ⌣ Sulphuric Acid
- ⌣ Dry Ice

80. In astronomy, the three bright stars in the constellation Orion are collectively known by what name?
- ⌣ Orion's Smile
- ⌣ Orion's Belt
- ⌣ Orion's Sock

81. Which part of the human body is most visibly affected by cellulite?
- ⌣ Skin
- ⌣ Nails
- ⌣ Hair

82. The glycaemic index is a system of classifying food based on the effect which food group has on blood glucose levels?
- ⌣ Protein
- ⌣ Fats
- ⌣ Carbohydrates

83. From what is the substance camphor derived?
- ⌣ Coal
- ⌣ Trees
- ⌣ Clay

84. The kiang, native to Tibet, belongs to which family of mammals?
- ⌣ Horse
- ⌣ Buffalo
- ⌣ Wolf

ANSWERS ON P.279

85. In what part of the human body would you find the vomer bone?
- ⌐⌐ Foot
- ⌐⌐ Chest
- ⌐⌐ Head

86. Which term refers to something that can be decomposed by bacteria or other living organisms?
- ⌐⌐ Biodiversity
- ⌐⌐ Biotecture
- ⌐⌐ Biodegradable

87. Tanning is a process used in the treatment of which material?
- ⌐⌐ Wool
- ⌐⌐ Leather
- ⌐⌐ Paper

88. The most common soft solders for joining metals are normally alloys of lead and which other metal?
- ⌐⌐ Tin
- ⌐⌐ Aluminium
- ⌐⌐ Nickel

89. Which planet, with an equatorial diameter of approximately 49,000km, is very similar in size to Uranus?
- ⌐⌐ Neptune
- ⌐⌐ Saturn
- ⌐⌐ Jupiter

90. The prehistoric *Dunkleosteus terrelli*, which scientists discovered in 2006 had a very powerful bite, was what type of creature?
- ⌐⌐ Reptile
- ⌐⌐ Fish
- ⌐⌐ Mammal

ANSWERS ON P.279

91. If an egg is rotten, what will it do when it is carefully lowered in its shell into a bowl of water?
  ⌐ Float to the Surface
  ⌐ Become Paler
  ⌐ Sink to the Bottom

92. Goliath frogs, which can grow to over one foot long, are indigenous to which continent?
  ⌐ South America
  ⌐ Africa
  ⌐ Asia

93. Which heavenly body was the destination of NASA's series of 'Ranger' missions?
  ⌐ Moon
  ⌐ Venus
  ⌐ Mars

94. Which Nobel Prize for Physics winner, who died in 1984, succeeded Sir Richard Woolley as Astronomer Royal in 1972?
  ⌐ Frank Dyson
  ⌐ Arnold Wolfendale
  ⌐ Martin Ryle

95. Pewter is typically an alloy of tin and which other metal?
  ⌐ Potassium
  ⌐ Lead
  ⌐ Magnesium

96. Thermodynamics is the study of the relation between various forms of energy and what?
  ⌐ Motion
  ⌐ Heat
  ⌐ Light

ANSWERS ON P.279

97. What natural phenomenon occurs when sunlight refracts through raindrops?
- ⊔ Cloud
- ⊔ Thunder
- ⊔ Rainbow

98. What colour is the halogen bromine, the only non-metallic element that is a liquid at room temperature?
- ⊔ Dark Blue
- ⊔ Dark Red
- ⊔ Dark Green

99. Which bird can be identified by its piercing 'teacher-teacher' song?
- ⊔ Great Tit
- ⊔ Robin
- ⊔ Chaffinch

100. In an isosceles triangle, how many sides are the same length?
- ⊔ None
- ⊔ Two
- ⊔ Three

ANSWERS ON P.279

GENERAL KNOWLEDGE

1. The actress Demi Moore married which actor in 1987?
   - ⊔ Sylvester Stallone
   - ⊔ Arnold Schwarzenegger
   - ⊔ Bruce Willis

2. Which US state is known as the 'Land of Lincoln'?
   - ⊔ Illinois
   - ⊔ California
   - ⊔ Indiana

3. Which London area is sometimes referred to as Banglatown?
   - ⊔ Camden Market
   - ⊔ Isle of Dogs
   - ⊔ Brick Lane

4. *La Danse*, featuring five naked forms dancing in a circle, is a 1909 work by which artist?
   - ⊔ Matisse
   - ⊔ Dali
   - ⊔ Duchamp

5. The fandango is a dance traditionally accompanied by what percussion instrument?
   - ⊔ Bongos
   - ⊔ Castanets
   - ⊔ Tambourine

6. Which Wiltshire town has been renowned for its carpets since a Royal Carpet Factory was built there in 1655?
   - ⊔ Chiseldon
   - ⊔ Pewsey
   - ⊔ Wilton

ANSWERS ON P.280

7. In Greek mythology, the Nereids, the fifty daughters of the god Nereus, are especially associated with what?
   - ⊔ Sea
   - ⊔ Mountains
   - ⊔ Flowers

8. Which character in Shakespeare's *Romeo and Juliet* delivers the famous 'Queen Mab' speech?
   - ⊔ Benvolio
   - ⊔ Tybalt
   - ⊔ Mercutio

9. Who in their professional work would be most likely to execute a 'do-si-do'?
   - ⊔ Sculptor
   - ⊔ Pianist
   - ⊔ Dancer

10. For what does the letter 'U' stand in the acronym SCUBA?
   - ⊔ Underground
   - ⊔ Underwater
   - ⊔ Underneath

11. What name is traditionally given to the puppeteer who performs a Punch and Judy show?
   - ⊔ Prophet
   - ⊔ Professor
   - ⊔ Provender

12. Which expression is often used when each person pays their own expenses on a date or outing?
   - ⊔ Go Dutch
   - ⊔ Go French
   - ⊔ Go German

ANSWERS ON P.280

13. In Greek mythology, which god is the patron of thieves and merchants and the protector of travellers?
  ⊔ Poseidon
  ⊔ Hermes
  ⊔ Dionysus

14. What name is given to a Scottish parish minister's house?
  ⊔ Manse
  ⊔ Midden
  ⊔ Bothy

15. The word 'sylvan' pertains to what kind of landscape?
  ⊔ Coastal
  ⊔ Woodland
  ⊔ Mountain

16. Who was chairman of the National Coal Board during its bitter fight with striking miners in 1984?
  ⊔ Ian MacGregor
  ⊔ Alistair McAlpine
  ⊔ Angus Ogilvy

17. In which city did Britain's first marmalade factory open in the late 18th century?
  ⊔ Glasgow
  ⊔ Aberdeen
  ⊔ Dundee

18. Maipo Valley and Casablanca Valley are wine-growing areas in which country?
  ⊔ Chile
  ⊔ South Africa
  ⊔ USA

ANSWERS ON P.280

19. Hangul is the alphabet or writing system of which language?
- Korean
- Farsi
- Basque

20. The Pyramid Stage is an integral feature of which music and arts festival which usually takes place in June in Somerset?
- Glastonbury
- Glyndebourne
- WOMAD

21. Alfred Wainwright devoted much of his life to mapping and describing which area of the British Isles?
- Snowdonia
- South Downs
- Lake District

22. In which city do the Dutch football team Feyenoord play their home games?
- Rotterdam
- Arnhem
- Utrecht

23. The four-weight World Champion boxer Manny Pacquiao was born in 1978 in which country?
- Mexico
- Cuba
- Philippines

24. Who was the president of the United States at the turn of the 20th century?
- Theodore Roosevelt
- William McKinley
- William Taft

ANSWERS ON P.280

25. Norman Parkinson, who married the actress Wenda Rogerson in 1947, was a famous name in which field?
- ⊔ Photography
- ⊔ Gardening
- ⊔ Politics

26. The long-running cartoon strip called *The Broons* is about a family from which of the UK's nations?
- ⊔ Scotland
- ⊔ Wales
- ⊔ England

27. What name is given to a person or thing that seems powerful but is in fact feeble?
- ⊔ Paper Wolf
- ⊔ Paper Tiger
- ⊔ Paper Shark

28. What name refers to a secluded building used for religious retreat or instruction in Hinduism?
- ⊔ Ashram
- ⊔ Samsara
- ⊔ Brahmin

29. In classical architecture, what type of column is characterised by a capital decorated with a scroll-like design called a 'volute'?
- ⊔ Doric
- ⊔ Ionic
- ⊔ Corinthian

30. Which comedian danced naked around Piccadilly Circus to raise money for Comic Relief in 2001?
- ⊔ Billy Connolly
- ⊔ Eddie Izzard
- ⊔ Lenny Henry

ANSWERS ON P.280

31. Manny Shinwell, who died in 1986, was a mainstay of which political party?
- ⊔ Conservative
- ⊔ Labour
- ⊔ Liberal

32. Typography is the design and layout of what?
- ⊔ Printed Words
- ⊔ Coloured Glass
- ⊔ Dried Flowers

33. The word 'angst', meaning a feeling of deep anxiety or dread, is thought to be derived from which language?
- ⊔ Italian
- ⊔ Russian
- ⊔ German

34. Charles Hardin were the real first names of which American singer?
- ⊔ Elvis Presley
- ⊔ Roy Orbison
- ⊔ Buddy Holly

35. D.H. Lawrence was known in his family by what diminutive name?
- ⊔ Fred
- ⊔ Mo
- ⊔ Bert

36. In military terminology, what name is given to a projection of the forward line into enemy territory?
- ⊔ Salient
- ⊔ Echelon
- ⊔ Melee

ANSWERS ON P.280

37. So-called 'Purbeck marble' is a type of which rock?
⌐ Slate
⌐ Granite
⌐ Limestone

38. Flinders Street station is the central railway station of which Australian city?
⌐ Melbourne
⌐ Sydney
⌐ Perth

39. As what did Irving Penn become well known in the 20th century?
⌐ Architect
⌐ Photographer
⌐ Musician

40. According to the nursery rhyme beginning 'Monday's Child ...', the baby born on which day has 'far to go'?
⌐ Monday
⌐ Thursday
⌐ Saturday

41. What name is given to unsolicited and unwanted emails?
⌐ Spam
⌐ Cookie
⌐ Chip

42. Which architect famously described a house as 'a machine for living in'?
⌐ Walter Gropius
⌐ Antoni Gaudí
⌐ Le Corbusier

ANSWERS ON P.280

43. What does the Yiddish term 'kvetch' mean?
- ⌐ To Complain
- ⌐ To Laugh
- ⌐ To Sleep

44. 'Glory be to God for dappled things' is the opening line of the poem 'Pied Beauty' by which writer?
- ⌐ Gerard Manley Hopkins
- ⌐ Samuel Taylor Coleridge
- ⌐ Edgar Allan Poe

45. Who traditionally reads the prayers that begin a sitting in the House of Commons?
- ⌐ Prime Minister
- ⌐ Speaker's Chaplain
- ⌐ Home Secretary

46. The cookery writer and presenter Rachel Allen was born in which country?
- ⌐ Ireland
- ⌐ New Zealand
- ⌐ South Africa

47. 'Pot' and 'Pearl' are types of which foodstuff?
- ⌐ Lentils
- ⌐ Pea
- ⌐ Barley

48. Which physical recreation movement was founded in England by Mary Bagot Stack in 1930?
- ⌐ Women's League of Health and Beauty
- ⌐ Women's Land Army
- ⌐ Women's Freedom League

ANSWERS ON P.280

49. The Watford Gap is located in which English county?
- ⊔ Northamptonshire
- ⊔ Oxfordshire
- ⊔ Bedfordshire

50. Which creatures are most commonly affected by 'Newcastle disease'?
- ⊔ Birds
- ⊔ Cows
- ⊔ Dogs

51. The TV series *Ashes to Ashes* and *Life on Mars* take their names from top ten hit singles by which singer?
- ⊔ David Bowie
- ⊔ Elton John
- ⊔ Paul Young

52. In the military, what name was sometimes given to a soldier assigned to an officer as a personal servant?
- ⊔ Superman
- ⊔ Batman
- ⊔ Spiderman

53. Where was the infamous WWI spy Mata Hari born?
- ⊔ Netherlands
- ⊔ Nigeria
- ⊔ Nicaragua

54. Italian industrialists the Agnelli family have been involved since 1923 with which Italian football club?
- ⊔ Juventus
- ⊔ AC Milan
- ⊔ Roma

ANSWERS ON P.280

55. Inaugurated by US Senator Gaylord Nelson in 1970, what is celebrated each year on the 22nd of April?
- ⌐ International Women's Day
- ⌐ Martin Luther King's Birthday
- ⌐ Earth Day

56. A statue of the Sylvester Stallone film character Rocky stands outside the Museum of Art in which American city?
- ⌐ Baltimore
- ⌐ Philadelphia
- ⌐ Detroit

57. Popular in the 16th and 17th centuries, the pavane is an example of what?
- ⌐ Poem
- ⌐ Collar
- ⌐ Dance

58. The new building of the British Library, which was completed in 1997, is immediately adjacent to which London mainline railway station?
- ⌐ Paddington
- ⌐ Victoria
- ⌐ St Pancras

59. Which renowned poet lived in a riverside villa at Twickenham where he created a famous grotto and gardens?
- ⌐ Jonathan Swift
- ⌐ Alexander Pope
- ⌐ Alfred, Lord Tennyson

60. Joshua Nkomo was an important figure in the politics of which country, spending several years as one of its vice presidents?
- ⌐ Lesotho
- ⌐ Kenya
- ⌐ Zimbabwe

ANSWERS ON P.280

61. Who directed the 2000 film *What Lies Beneath*?
- ⊔ Barry Levinson
- ⊔ Mike Figgis
- ⊔ Robert Zemeckis

62. *De Telegraaf* and *Algemeen Dagblad* are national daily newspapers in which country?
- ⊔ Netherlands
- ⊔ Austria
- ⊔ Germany

63. 'Jueves' is the Spanish name for which day of the week?
- ⊔ Monday
- ⊔ Tuesday
- ⊔ Thursday

64. How many squares are there on a traditional Scrabble board?
- ⊔ 225
- ⊔ 289
- ⊔ 400

65. On a standard QWERTY keyboard, what letter is situated between A and D?
- ⊔ F
- ⊔ S
- ⊔ L

66. Which then-daring fashion item was invented and first displayed by the Frenchman Louis Réard in 1946?
- ⊔ Bikini
- ⊔ Leotard
- ⊔ Thong

ANSWERS ON P.280

67. Before he became a comedian and TV personality Harry Hill underwent training to become what?
    - ⊔ Lawyer
    - ⊔ Doctor
    - ⊔ Policeman

68. In Roman mythology, who was the god of the sun?
    - ⊔ Selene
    - ⊔ Sol
    - ⊔ Saturn

69. Which political philosopher was born in Trier in 1818 and died in London in 1883?
    - ⊔ Jean-Jacques Rousseau
    - ⊔ Friedrich Nietzsche
    - ⊔ Karl Marx

70. What, according to the famous 1960s comment by the Canadian communications theorist Marshall McLuhan, 'is the message'?
    - ⊔ The Memory
    - ⊔ The Medium
    - ⊔ The Monitor

71. 'The horror! The horror!' are the famous last words of a main character in which of Joseph Conrad's works?
    - ⊔ Lord Jim
    - ⊔ The Secret Agent
    - ⊔ Heart of Darkness

72. A cappuccino in Italy served 'senza schiuma' doesn't have what?
    - ⊔ Froth
    - ⊔ Cocoa Powder
    - ⊔ Sugar

ANSWERS ON P.280

73. In which country did the 1937 Hindenburg airship disaster occur?
- ⊔ Germany
- ⊔ USA
- ⊔ UK

74. Which popular carbohydrate restricting diet takes its name from an area of Miami Beach?
- ⊔ North Beach
- ⊔ South Beach
- ⊔ West Beach

75. What name is given to the Jewish plaited loaf traditionally eaten on the Sabbath?
- ⊔ Babka
- ⊔ Matzo
- ⊔ Challah

76. Which philosopher wrote the 1943 work *Being and Nothingness*?
- ⊔ Jean-Paul Sartre
- ⊔ Bertrand Russell
- ⊔ Ludwig Wittgenstein

77. The French singer Charles Aznavour had a UK number one hit in 1974 with which song?
- ⊔ He
- ⊔ She
- ⊔ We

78. Which word is used to describe an agreement or series of negotiations that are undertaken by two countries or states?
- ⊔ Unilateral
- ⊔ Bilateral
- ⊔ Multilateral

ANSWERS ON P.280

79. Whose 1933 novel *Love on the Dole* chronicled working class poverty in Northern England?
- ⌣ Walter Greenwood
- ⌣ Christopher Isherwood
- ⌣ Evelyn Waugh

80. The Tora Bora cave complex is situated in which country?
- ⌣ Afghanistan
- ⌣ Thailand
- ⌣ Egypt

81. The French-named egg dish 'oeufs en cocotte' is often served in which receptacle?
- ⌣ Ramekin
- ⌣ Teacup
- ⌣ Tagine

82. What type of aircraft was the Sopwith Camel?
- ⌣ Glider
- ⌣ Helicopter
- ⌣ Biplane

83. Rosh Hashanah marks the start of the new year in which religion?
- ⌣ Judaism
- ⌣ Christianity
- ⌣ Islam

84. What is the mathematical term for the corner point of a triangle or pyramid?
- ⌣ Cortex
- ⌣ Reflex
- ⌣ Vertex

ANSWERS ON P.280

85. What type of architectural feature is an 'oeil-de-boeuf'?
- Niche
- Staircase
- Window

86. Which letter in Morse code is represented by the pattern dot-dot-dot-dash?
- U
- V
- W

87. 'Pink Lady' is a variety of which fruit?
- Apple
- Orange
- Pear

88. Which female singer had 1980s top ten UK hit singles with 'Buffalo Stance' and 'Manchild'?
- Lisa Stansfield
- Neneh Cherry
- Enya

89. What name is often given to wisps of trailing cirrus clouds?
- Crow's Nests
- Pig's Ears
- Mare's Tails

90. How many Tate galleries are there in the UK?
- 2
- 3
- 4

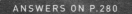 ANSWERS ON P.280

91. Which film director, whose movies include *Ray* and *An Officer and a Gentleman*, married Helen Mirren in 1997?
- ⊔ Peter Weir
- ⊔ John Madden
- ⊔ Taylor Hackford

92. The Mishna is a collection of legal traditions and moral precepts that forms part of which religion?
- ⊔ Judaism
- ⊔ Islam
- ⊔ Hinduism

93. Danny Amatullo, Lydia Grant and Coco Hernandez were all characters in which 1980s US TV series?
- ⊔ Fame
- ⊔ LA Law
- ⊔ Cagney and Lacey

94. The Premier League footballers Petr ech and José Reina play in which position?
- ⊔ Goalkeeper
- ⊔ Defender
- ⊔ Striker

95. Trevor Phillips was appointed the head of which organisation in 2006?
- ⊔ Amnesty International
- ⊔ Metropolitan Police
- ⊔ Equality and Human Rights Commission

96. What breed of dog did Senator Ted Kennedy give to the children of Barack Obama in April 2009?
- ⊔ Hungarian Vizsla
- ⊔ Portuguese Water Dog
- ⊔ Rhodesian Ridgeback

ANSWERS ON P.280

97. Clive Stafford Smith is acclaimed for his work in which field?
⊔ Law
⊔ Business
⊔ Advertising

98. Which nursery rhyme character 'stepped in a puddle, right up to his middle'?
⊔ Jack Sprat
⊔ Doctor Foster
⊔ Solomon Grundy

99. The United States celebrated its Bicentennial on the 4th of July of which year?
⊔ 1976
⊔ 1986
⊔ 1996

100. Which singer launched perfumes called 'Miss You Nights' and 'Dream Maker'?
⊔ Cliff Richard
⊔ Tony Bennett
⊔ Lionel Richie

ANSWERS ON P.280

CHRIS HUGHES

FULL NAME:
Christopher John Hughes

HOME TOWN:
Crewe. (Previously Enfield, Middlesex.)

EDUCATION:
Up to GCE O-level (Enfield Grammar School 1958–62. Expelled)

QUIZZING CREDENTIALS:
Mastermind 1983, *Brain of Britain* 2005.

LEAST FAVOURITE SUBJECT:
Sport. This is not a 'subject' in my scheme of things – it's just list-learning and trivia.

SPECIAL INTEREST:
Railway history, steam technology, maritime history, transport history in general.

HOBBIES:
Currently building 4mm scale models of old London buses, from the NS of 1923 to the post-war RT of 1947.

WHAT DOES IT TAKE TO BE AN EGGHEAD:
A strange mind and a refusal to be intimidated by the glamour of television.

ULTIMATE QUIZ TEAM:
Kevin Ashman (of course), Stephen Fry, the late, great Magnus Magnusson, Victoria Mitchell-Coren, Sheldon Cooper (from *The Big Bang Theory*) and, in reserve, Carol Vorderman.

MOST MEMORABLE MOMENT:
The entire *Eggheads* team almost losing in sudden death to, of all people, Jade Goody. (This was before she fell so tragically ill.)

ADVICE FOR BUDDING EGGHEADS:
Don't just 'know' stuff, *understand* it, and realise that everything is connected, however tenuously. Also don't dismiss anything (except sport) as 'boring'.

FAVOURITE FACT:
All facts are good, provided you can separate them from myths.

LITTLE KNOWN FACT:
At the wedding of Prince Andrew and Sarah Ferguson, I was on duty as a Special Constable, and it was I, with my right arm locked into the balustrade of South Africa Gate, and my left arm round the waist of a tiny WPC, who formed the anchor of the police line holding back the crowds outside Buckingham Palace.

1. **Kate Winslet, Patrick Stewart and Orlando Bloom all appeared in which TV comedy series?**
   - ⊔ Extras
   - ⊔ Men Behaving Badly
   - ⊔ The League of Gentlemen

2. **The TV series *The Royal* was mainly set in what type of establishment?**
   - ⊔ Hospital
   - ⊔ Pub
   - ⊔ Hotel

3. **Who provides the voice of the super villain 'Megamind' in the 2010 film of the same name?**
   - ⊔ Will Ferrell
   - ⊔ Michael Keaton
   - ⊔ Steve Carell

4. **Which *Friends* actor played the character Herbert Sobel in the 2001 TV series *Band of Brothers*?**
   - ⊔ David Schwimmer
   - ⊔ Matt LeBlanc
   - ⊔ Matthew Perry

5. **The film director Peter Weir was born in which country in 1944?**
   - ⊔ Australia
   - ⊔ New Zealand
   - ⊔ India

6. **Maggie Smith received the first Oscar nomination of her career for her performance in which 1965 film?**
   - ⊔ The Prime of Miss Jean Brodie
   - ⊔ Othello
   - ⊔ Oh! What a Lovely War

ANSWERS ON P.281

7. What was the name of the character played by Judi Dench
   in the TV drama series *Cranford*?
   ⊔ Miss Octavia Pole
   ⊔ Miss Augusta Tomkinson
   ⊔ Miss Matty Jenkyns

8. Who played the title role in the 2001 comedy film *Mike
   Bassett: England Manager*?
   ⊔ Warren Clarke
   ⊔ Ricky Tomlinson
   ⊔ John Thomson

9. Which actor played the character Goose in the film *Top Gun*
   and Dr Greene in the hospital drama *ER*?
   ⊔ Anthony Edwards
   ⊔ Eriq La Salle
   ⊔ George Clooney

10. Who provided the voice for Scrooge in the 2009 animated
    film *A Christmas Carol*?
    ⊔ Jim Carrey
    ⊔ Tom Hanks
    ⊔ Mike Myers

11. Which former Spice Girl joined the judging panel of *Dancing
    on Ice* in 2010?
    ⊔ Geri Halliwell
    ⊔ Melanie Chisholm
    ⊔ Emma Bunton

12. On which street did Hyacinth Bucket live in the TV sitcom
    Keeping Up Appearances?
    ⊔ Wisteria Lane
    ⊔ Blossom Avenue
    ⊔ Magnolia Crescent

ANSWERS ON P.281

13. Who was the star of the 1963 film *It Happened at the World's Fair*?
   ⊔ Elvis Presley
   ⊔ Judy Garland
   ⊔ James Cagney

14. In the 1951 film *The Lavender Hill Mob*, the stolen gold bullion is moulded into miniature souvenir versions of which landmark?
   ⊔ Eiffel Tower
   ⊔ Leaning Tower of Pisa
   ⊔ Statue of Liberty

15. Who won a BAFTA award for his portrayal of the scientist John Harrison in the 2000 TV drama *Longitude*?
   ⊔ Ben Kingsley
   ⊔ John Hurt
   ⊔ Michael Gambon

16. In the US TV soap *Dallas*, what was the name of the father of JR and Bobby Ewing?
   ⊔ Mitch
   ⊔ Chuck
   ⊔ Jock

17. Who played Doctor Richard Burke, a romantic interest for Monica, in the US TV comedy *Friends*?
   ⊔ Ted Danson
   ⊔ Steve Guttenberg
   ⊔ Tom Selleck

18. For what does the letter 'C' stand in the name of the news channel CNN?
   ⊔ Cable
   ⊔ Continuous
   ⊔ Commercial

ANSWERS ON P.281

19. Michelle Yeoh played Wai Lin in which James Bond film?
 ⌴ Tomorrow Never Dies
 ⌴ Die Another Day
 ⌴ GoldenEye

20. In the 1967 film *The Graduate*, when Mr McGuire tells Benjamin that he just wants to say one word to him, what is that word?
 ⌴ Plastics
 ⌴ Oil
 ⌴ Insurance

21. Which seaside resort is the name of a 2004 TV drama series starring David Morrissey and David Tennant?
 ⌴ Redcar
 ⌴ Newquay
 ⌴ Blackpool

22. Who played the bumbling policeman Frank Drebin in the *Police Squad* TV series and in the *Naked Gun* film series?
 ⌴ Leslie Nielsen
 ⌴ Steve Martin
 ⌴ James Belushi

23. In the historical detective TV series, Brother Cadfael is a monk at which monastic house?
 ⌴ York Minster
 ⌴ Shrewsbury Abbey
 ⌴ Lindisfarne

24. The 1980s soap opera *The Colbys* was a spin-off from which other programme?
 ⌴ Dallas
 ⌴ Dynasty
 ⌴ Falcon Crest

ANSWERS ON P.281

25. The long-running crime drama *A Touch of Frost*, starring
    David Jason, is based in which fictional town?
    ⊔ Denton
    ⊔ Cardale
    ⊔ Tarrant

26. Which French actor was the star of the 1960s film *Le
    Samouraï*?
    ⊔ Jean-Paul Belmondo
    ⊔ Alain Delon
    ⊔ Gérard Depardieu

27. In 1994, Barbara Windsor joined the cast of *EastEnders*
    playing which character?
    ⊔ Pauline Fowler
    ⊔ Angie Watts
    ⊔ Peggy Mitchell

28. The twins John and Edward Grimes found fame on which TV
    show in 2009?
    ⊔ Britain's Got Talent
    ⊔ The X Factor
    ⊔ Big Brother

29. To which continent do the characters Carl and Russell
    travel in the 2009 film *Up*?
    ⊔ Africa
    ⊔ Asia
    ⊔ South America

30. Which film director did Sofia Coppola marry in 1999?
    ⊔ David O Russell
    ⊔ Spike Jonze
    ⊔ Wes Anderson

ANSWERS ON P.281

31. In which year was *Only Fools and Horses* first broadcast on British television?
  ⊔ 1975
  ⊔ 1978
  ⊔ 1981

32. Ted Rogers was the host of which popular game show?
  ⊔ 3-2-1
  ⊔ Mr & Mrs
  ⊔ Family Fortunes

33. 'I'll get you, my pretty, and your little dog too!' is a quote from which 1939 film?
  ⊔ Gone With the Wind
  ⊔ The Wizard of Oz
  ⊔ The Hunchback of Notre Dame

34. George Clooney starred as Lyn Cassady in the 2009 film *The Men Who Stare at . . .* what?
  ⊔ Horses
  ⊔ Goats
  ⊔ Cows

35. Who was the first presenter of the 1970s children's TV film quiz *Screen Test*?
  ⊔ John Craven
  ⊔ Michael Rodd
  ⊔ Michael Buerk

36. Which actress was nominated for an Oscar for her role in the 1945 film *Leave Her to Heaven*?
  ⊔ Gene Tierney
  ⊔ Veronica Lake
  ⊔ Lana Turner

ANSWERS ON P.281

37. Who provided the voice of 'Badger' in the 2009 film *Fantastic Mr Fox*?
   ⏄ Michael Gambon
   ⏄ Willem Dafoe
   ⏄ Bill Murray

38. Which tennis player took part in the 2009 series of the TV show *Strictly Come Dancing*?
   ⏄ Steffi Graf
   ⏄ Martina Hingis
   ⏄ Venus Williams

39. What is the title of the TV talk show created in 2000 and hosted by Matthew Wright?
   ⏄ The Wright Stuff
   ⏄ The Wright One
   ⏄ The Wright Way

40. Who played the title role in the 1967 film *Dr Dolittle*?
   ⏄ Rex Harrison
   ⏄ Dick Van Dyke
   ⏄ Bing Crosby

41. Who provides the voice of Marty the zebra in the Madagascar series of films?
   ⏄ John Goodman
   ⏄ Tim Allen
   ⏄ Chris Rock

42. What is the name of the red setter-dachshund cross that became a *Blue Peter* pet in 2009?
   ⏄ Barney
   ⏄ Bodger
   ⏄ Baggy

ANSWERS ON P.281

43. Which TV programme did Jimmy Hill join as a regular presenter in 1973?
- ⌙ Panorama
- ⌙ Gardeners' World
- ⌙ Match of the Day

44. Which comedy double act starred in the 1960s sketch show *Not Only ... But Also*?
- ⌙ Peter Cook and Dudley Moore
- ⌙ The Two Ronnies
- ⌙ Tony Hancock and Sid James

45. Joe Pesci and Daniel Stern play burglars Harry and Marv in which US comedy film?
- ⌙ Home Alone
- ⌙ Home for the Holidays
- ⌙ A Home of Our Own

46. Who is the main character in the 1964 film *A Shot in the Dark*?
- ⌙ Hercule Poirot
- ⌙ Inspector Clouseau
- ⌙ Harry Palmer

47. Which tennis player was the host of both the American and British versions of the television gameshow *The Chair* in 2002?
- ⌙ Boris Becker
- ⌙ John McEnroe
- ⌙ Pat Cash

48. The TV comedy series *Green Wing* is set in which type of establishment?
- ⌙ Fire Station
- ⌙ Hospital
- ⌙ Snooker Hall

ANSWERS ON P.281

49. Who was nominated for an Oscar for his role as 'Red' Redding in the 1994 film *The Shawshank Redemption*?
- ⊔ Denzel Washington
- ⊔ Samuel L Jackson
- ⊔ Morgan Freeman

50. What is the name of Nessa and Smithy's baby in the TV sitcom *Gavin and Stacey*?
- ⊔ Harry
- ⊔ Brian
- ⊔ Neil

51. Who directed the 2009 science fiction film *Avatar*?
- ⊔ James Cameron
- ⊔ Ron Howard
- ⊔ Robert Zemeckis

52. What was the title of Alfred Hitchcock's penultimate film, with a cast including Jon Finch, Alec McCowen and Billie Whitelaw?
- ⊔ Frantic
- ⊔ Fury
- ⊔ Frenzy

53. Sue Johnston, plays a character called Barbara in which TV sitcom?
- ⊔ Gavin and Stacey
- ⊔ The IT Crowd
- ⊔ The Royle Family

54. In 2009, which TV presenter starred in a TV series in which he built a house made entirely of Lego and a garden made entirely of Plasticine?
- ⊔ James May
- ⊔ Stephen Fry
- ⊔ Vernon Kay

ANSWERS ON P.281

55. Which former newsreader was the host of the 1980s programme *Treasure Hunt*?
   ⌐ Reginald Bosanquet
   ⌐ Richard Baker
   ⌐ Kenneth Kendall

56. Jason Voorhees is the major recurring character in which ongoing series of horror films?
   ⌐ Halloween
   ⌐ Friday the 13th
   ⌐ Scream

57. Which English comedian appeared in the films *There's Something About Mary*, *The Fifth Element* and *The Ladies Man*?
   ⌐ Lee Evans
   ⌐ Alan Davies
   ⌐ Eddie Izzard

58. In 1994, which *Blackadder* actor became a regular presenter of the archaeology TV series *Time Team*?
   ⌐ Tony Robinson
   ⌐ Stephen Fry
   ⌐ Tim McInnerny

59. Jen, played by Katherine Parkinson, is a character in which TV sitcom?
   ⌐ The Inbetweeners
   ⌐ The Royle Family
   ⌐ The IT Crowd

60. *Freddy's Revenge* was the subtitle of the second film in which series?
   ⌐ A Nightmare on Elm Street
   ⌐ Halloween
   ⌐ Amityville

ANSWERS ON P.281

61. For what did the 'D' stand in the initials of the silent film director known as D.W. Griffith?
    ⊔ David
    ⊔ Daniel
    ⊔ Derek

62. Which American comic actor played 'Hercule Poirot' in the mid-1960s film *The Alphabet Murders*?
    ⊔ Gig Young
    ⊔ Tony Randall
    ⊔ Jack Lemmon

63. Bouncer the dog appeared regularly in which TV soap?
    ⊔ EastEnders
    ⊔ Dallas
    ⊔ Neighbours

64. Who hosted the TV game show *Play Your Cards Right* from 1980 to 1987 and then again in the 1990s?
    ⊔ Les Dawson
    ⊔ Bruce Forsyth
    ⊔ Bob Monkhouse

65. Which actor played the character known as 'Mr Big' in the US TV series *Sex and the City*?
    ⊔ Chris Noth
    ⊔ Patrick Dempsey
    ⊔ Matthew Fox

66. Which comedy film features the memorable line 'I'll have what she's having'?
    ⊔ Four Weddings and a Funeral
    ⊔ Pretty Woman
    ⊔ When Harry Met Sally

ANSWERS ON P.281

67. Who played Frankenstein's Monster in Kenneth Branagh's 1994 film version of Mary Shelley's novel?

  ⌴ Johnny Depp
  ⌴ Dustin Hoffman
  ⌴ Robert De Niro

68. Which TV series, first broadcast in 2009, centred on the lives of a group of Pre-Raphaelite artists?

  ⌴ Mistresses
  ⌴ Desperate Romantics
  ⌴ Ashes to Ashes

69. 23 Railway Cuttings was the address of a character played by which actor in a comedy series?

  ⌴ Ronnie Barker
  ⌴ Tony Hancock
  ⌴ Warren Mitchell

70. Who played Roger Bartlett, codenamed 'Big X', in the 1963 film *The Great Escape*?

  ⌴ Richard Attenborough
  ⌴ Steve McQueen
  ⌴ James Garner

71. The Borg and the Ferengi are alien races in which sci-fi television series?

  ⌴ Battlestar Galactica
  ⌴ Blake's 7
  ⌴ Star Trek: The Next Generation

72. Which former *Doctor Who* actor stars as the villain in the 2009 film *GI Joe: The Rise of Cobra*?

  ⌴ Peter Davison
  ⌴ Tom Baker
  ⌴ Christopher Eccleston

ANSWERS ON P.281

73. Who directed the films *Ferris Bueller's Day Off*, *Weird Science* and *The Breakfast Club*?
- ⊔ James Foley
- ⊔ John Hughes
- ⊔ Martin Brest

74. The 'Diary Room' is an important feature on the set of which reality TV show?
- ⊔ The Apprentice
- ⊔ Big Brother
- ⊔ Strictly Come Dancing

75. A film that tells someone's life story is commonly known as what?
- ⊔ Time-lapse
- ⊔ Biopic
- ⊔ Autofocus

76. *Whatever Works*, starring Larry David, is a 2009 film comedy by which director?
- ⊔ Nora Ephron
- ⊔ Rob Reiner
- ⊔ Woody Allen

77. What type of creatures are Bernard and Miss Bianca, the title characters of the Disney animated feature *The Rescuers*?
- ⊔ Dogs
- ⊔ Chimpanzees
- ⊔ Mice

78. *The Naked Civil Servant*, the 1975 TV film about Quentin Crisp starring John Hurt, was first broadcast on which channel?
- ⊔ BBC1
- ⊔ BBC2
- ⊔ ITV

ANSWERS ON P.281

79. Which actress has appeared in the films *The Italian Job*, *Hancock* and *The Cider House Rules*?
- ⊔ Nicole Kidman
- ⊔ Charlize Theron
- ⊔ Renée Zellweger

80. Cheryl Fergison joined the cast of which TV soap in 2007 playing Heather Trott?
- ⊔ EastEnders
- ⊔ Emmerdale
- ⊔ Coronation Street

81. Which actor played the role of Clive Candy in the Powell and Pressburger film *The Life and Death of Colonel Blimp*?
- ⊔ Peter Ustinov
- ⊔ Leslie Howard
- ⊔ Roger Livesey

82. Which film did Michael Bay direct after *Bad Boys* and prior to *Armageddon*?
- ⊔ The Island
- ⊔ Pearl Harbor
- ⊔ The Rock

83. In which TV drama series did the title character work for the 'Bureau des Étrangers'?
- ⊔ Shoestring
- ⊔ Taggart
- ⊔ Bergerac

84. The line 'I'm not bad; I'm just drawn that way' was spoken by which cartoon character in a 1988 film?
- ⊔ Betty Boop
- ⊔ Cruella de Vil
- ⊔ Jessica Rabbit

ANSWERS ON P.281

85. What is Alfred Hitchcock doing in his cameo appearance at the beginning of his 1963 film *The Birds*?
- ⏣ Stroking a Cat
- ⏣ Walking Dogs
- ⏣ Feeding Fish

86. The style of film and television animation called 'Anime' originated in which country?
- ⏣ Canada
- ⏣ Japan
- ⏣ Sweden

87. Which animator provided the voice for the character 'Bagpuss' in the children's TV series of the same name?
- ⏣ David McKee
- ⏣ Bob Godfrey
- ⏣ Oliver Postgate

88. Who played the role of Lady Marchmain in the 2008 film version of *Brideshead Revisited*?
- ⏣ Greta Scacchi
- ⏣ Emma Thompson
- ⏣ Kristin Scott Thomas

89. Which duo starred in the 1941 film *Buck Privates*?
- ⏣ Abbott and Costello
- ⏣ Martin and Lewis
- ⏣ Laurel and Hardy

90. Yabba-Dabba-Doo is a catchphrase of which cartoon character?
- ⏣ Yogi Bear
- ⏣ Hong Kong Phooey
- ⏣ Fred Flintstone

ANSWERS ON P.281

91. The four main characters in the 1980s TV series *The A-Team* were all veterans of which conflict?
    ⊔ World War II
    ⊔ Vietnam War
    ⊔ Korean War

92. Who played Hans Gruber in the 1988 film *Die Hard*?
    ⊔ Alan Rickman
    ⊔ Ralph Fiennes
    ⊔ Charles Dance

93. Dallas is the name of the captain of the main spacecraft in which science fiction film?
    ⊔ Alien
    ⊔ 2001: A Space Odyssey
    ⊔ Forbidden Planet

94. Which film actor was born Emmanuel Goldenberg in Bucharest and later became famous for his gangster roles?
    ⊔ James Cagney
    ⊔ George Raft
    ⊔ Edward G. Robinson

95. Who played British tennis player Peter Colt in the 2004 film *Wimbledon*?
    ⊔ Paul Bettany
    ⊔ Ioan Gruffudd
    ⊔ Daniel Day-Lewis

96. Percy Thrower appeared regularly on which children's show from 1974 until shortly before his death in 1988?
    ⊔ Play School
    ⊔ Blue Peter
    ⊔ Tiswas

ANSWERS ON P.281

97. Who appeared as Admiral Sir Edward Pellew in the TV series *Hornblower*?
- ⊔ Robert Lindsay
- ⊔ Michael Gambon
- ⊔ Edward Fox

98. Fred Gwynne is best known for his role as which 1960s TV comic character?
- ⊔ Gomez Addams
- ⊔ Uncle Fester
- ⊔ Herman Munster

99. Rose Nylund and Blanche Devereaux were two of the leading characters in which US TV show?
- ⊔ Northern Exposure
- ⊔ Family Ties
- ⊔ The Golden Girls

100. Which actor appeared in the films *Shutter Island*, *Zodiac* and *13 Going on 30* ?
- ⊔ Kevin Bacon
- ⊔ Mark Ruffalo
- ⊔ Gerard Butler

ANSWERS ON P.281

GENERAL KNOWLEDGE

1. What is the primary activity of a 'glee club'?
   - ⌵ Swimming
   - ⌵ Sewing
   - ⌵ Singing

2. 'Spondulicks' is a slang term for what?
   - ⌵ Money
   - ⌵ Time
   - ⌵ Health

3. Which member of the royal family married Baroness Marie-Christine von Reibnitz in Vienna in 1978?
   - ⌵ Prince Michael of Kent
   - ⌵ Duke of Gloucester
   - ⌵ Viscount Linley

4. Kara Zor-El is one of the names of which comic book superhero?
   - ⌵ Catwoman
   - ⌵ Supergirl
   - ⌵ Wonder Woman

5. The Boshin civil war took place in which country in the 19th century?
   - ⌵ Mexico
   - ⌵ Turkey
   - ⌵ Japan

6. The Johann Sebastian Bach work known as *The Goldberg Variations* was originally written for which musical instrument?
   - ⌵ Cello
   - ⌵ Cornet
   - ⌵ Harpsichord

ANSWERS ON P.282

7. The Venice Biennale is an art exhibition that takes place how often?
   - ⊔ Every Year
   - ⊔ Every Two Years
   - ⊔ Every Three Years

8. What astrological sign is normally represented by a pair of fishes?
   - ⊔ Pisces
   - ⊔ Aquarius
   - ⊔ Libra

9. What informal name is used to describe the steps that run through the middle of the benches in the House of Commons?
   - ⊔ Gantry
   - ⊔ Gangway
   - ⊔ Gangplank

10. Elinor Ostrom and Oliver Williamson jointly won a 2009 Nobel Prize in which field?
    - ⊔ Physics
    - ⊔ Medicine
    - ⊔ Economics

11. 'Potch' is an informal term for an inferior type of which stone?
    - ⊔ Opal
    - ⊔ Diamond
    - ⊔ Ruby

12. Which *Coronation Street* character was very proud of her so-called wall 'muriel' which featured flying ducks?
    - ⊔ Bet Lynch
    - ⊔ Annie Walker
    - ⊔ Hilda Ogden

ANSWERS ON P.282

13. 'Slow and steady wins the race' is the moral of which fable attributed to Aesop?
    ⊔ The Tortoise and the Hare
    ⊔ The Boy Who Cried Wolf
    ⊔ The Crow and the Pitcher

14. In Bananarama's hit 'Robert De Niro's Waiting', which language is the titular actor said to be 'talking'?
    ⊔ German
    ⊔ French
    ⊔ Italian

15. Louis Armstrong airport serves which US city?
    ⊔ New Orleans
    ⊔ Atlanta
    ⊔ Philadelphia

16. What type of wine is stored and matured in a heated chamber called an estufa?
    ⊔ Retsina
    ⊔ Madeira
    ⊔ Sake

17. An arboretum is a type of garden that is specifically devoted to the cultivation of which type of plants?
    ⊔ Orchids
    ⊔ Cacti
    ⊔ Trees

18. The prison called Wormwood Scrubs is in which city?
    ⊔ London
    ⊔ Manchester
    ⊔ Cardiff

ANSWERS ON P.282

19. Abebe Bikila won two Olympic gold medals in which athletics event in the 1960s?
    ⌴ High Jump
    ⌴ Marathon
    ⌴ 100 metres

20. Which term refers to items that have been deliberately thrown from ships, which then sink or are washed ashore?
    ⌴ Flotsam
    ⌴ Jetsam
    ⌴ Lagan

21. Paul Biya was re-elected in 2004 for a further seven years as President of which African country?
    ⌴ Cameroon
    ⌴ Nigeria
    ⌴ Ivory Coast

22. What is 'futhark'?
    ⌴ Traditional Inuit Medicine
    ⌴ Korean Martial Art
    ⌴ Runic Alphabet

23. Of which country is Utrecht both a city and a province?
    ⌴ Netherlands
    ⌴ Germany
    ⌴ Sweden

24. Which word describes the police action of managing large crowds by containing them in a limited area?
    ⌴ Cupping
    ⌴ Boiling
    ⌴ Kettling

ANSWERS ON P.282

25. The theme from Mike Oldfield's *Tubular Bells* famously featured on the soundtrack of which horror film?

- Halloween
- The Exorcist
- A Nightmare on Elm Street

26. In France, what is a 'Hotel de Ville'?

- Post Office
- Hospital
- Town Hall

27. What is the collective term for all the petals of a flower?

- Corona
- Corolla
- Corozo

28. What weapon does the title character use to kill the albatross in Coleridge's poem *The Rime of the Ancient Mariner*?

- Crossbow
- Sword
- Hammer

29. Gill Sans, designed in the 1920s by the English artist Eric Gill, is an example of what?

- Typeface
- Chair
- Pottery

30. The word 'leporine' means resembling or pertaining to which creature?

- Owl
- Donkey
- Hare

ANSWERS ON P.282

31. What is the job title given to the representatives of the Crown for each county of the UK?
   - ⊔ Lord-in-Waiting
   - ⊔ Lord of the Manor
   - ⊔ Lord Lieutenant

32. Which is the lowest-ranking type of admiral in the Royal Navy?
   - ⊔ Admiral of the Fleet
   - ⊔ Rear-Admiral
   - ⊔ Vice-Admiral

33. Who wrote the 1970s sci-fi novel *A Scanner Darkly*, later adapted for the cinema?
   - ⊔ Philip K. Dick
   - ⊔ Isaac Asimov
   - ⊔ Douglas Adams

34. What type of animal was Chi Chi, one of the star attractions at London Zoo from 1958 until her death in 1972?
   - ⊔ Giant Panda
   - ⊔ White Tiger
   - ⊔ Pygmy Hippo

35. According to the common saying, 'in the country of the blind, the one-eyed man is ...' what?
   - ⊔ Blessed
   - ⊔ Rare
   - ⊔ King

36. In South America, what is a 'gaucho'?
   - ⊔ Politician
   - ⊔ Cowboy
   - ⊔ Doctor

ANSWERS ON P.282

37. In entomological terms, what is a fritillary?
- Bee
- Ladybird
- Butterfly

38. 'Break Your Heart' was a UK number one single for which singer in September 2009?
- Dizzee Rascal
- Tinchy Stryder
- Taio Cruz

39. What colour is the top horizontal stripe on the national flags of Serbia, Paraguay and Croatia?
- Red
- White
- Blue

40. Which foodstuff appears on French menus as 'Épinards'?
- Spinach
- Mushrooms
- Cauliflower

41. D'Oyly Carte Island is situated in which British river?
- Severn
- Thames
- Avon

42. Christopher Tookey, Philip French and Mark Kermode are established critics of which of the arts?
- Dance
- Literature
- Film

ANSWERS ON P.282

43. The film director Duncan Jones, whose debut feature *Moon* was released in 2009, is the son of which musician?
- ⌴ Sting
- ⌴ David Bowie
- ⌴ Bryan Ferry

44. Which comedy actor had the fictional boss 'Mr Grimsdale'?
- ⌴ Peter Sellers
- ⌴ Terry Scott
- ⌴ Norman Wisdom

45. F. Scott Fitzgerald's second novel is entitled *The Beautiful and ... *what?
- ⌴ Dutiful
- ⌴ Desperate
- ⌴ Damned

46. Former pupils of the English public school Stowe are known as what?
- ⌴ Old Stovers
- ⌴ Old Stowaways
- ⌴ Old Stoics

47. Which Stanley Kubrick war film is based on Gustav Hasford's novel *The Short Timers*?
- ⌴ Paths of Glory
- ⌴ Full Metal Jacket
- ⌴ Dr Strangelove

48. *Rodong Sinmun* is the name of the official daily Communist newspaper of which country?
- ⌴ Burma
- ⌴ North Korea
- ⌴ Albania

ANSWERS ON P.282

49. In Germany, what is a 'Flughafen'?
- ⌴ Motorway
- ⌴ Airport
- ⌴ Library

50. Considered sacred by the Aztecs, what type of creature is the quetzal?
- ⌴ Bird
- ⌴ Cougar
- ⌴ Cayman

51. Who played the title role in the 2008 TV drama *Filth: The Mary Whitehouse Story*?
- ⌴ Celia Imrie
- ⌴ Victoria Wood
- ⌴ Julie Walters

52. Which US city is home to the Cedars-Sinai hospital?
- ⌴ New York
- ⌴ Dallas
- ⌴ Los Angeles

53. Which Irish singer attracted international criticism after tearing up a picture of Pope John Paul II live on American TV in 1992?
- ⌴ Bono
- ⌴ Bob Geldof
- ⌴ Sinead O'Connor

54. Which part of a mechanical clock has types that include verge, anchor, deadbeat and grasshopper?
- ⌴ Gear Train
- ⌴ Escapement
- ⌴ Pendulum

ANSWERS ON P.282

55. Three colleges in the University of Cambridge, Murray Edwards, Newnham and Lucy Cavendish, admit only who as students?
- ⊔ Women
- ⊔ Non-UK Residents
- ⊔ Former State School Pupils

56. What name is given to the slightly raised area at the front of an English equestrian saddle?
- ⊔ Pommel
- ⊔ Cantle
- ⊔ Tree

57. A famous hymn by Charles Wesley is called 'Love divine, all loves . . .' what?
- ⊔ Foretelling
- ⊔ Excelling
- ⊔ Compelling

58. The expression 'namby-pamby', meaning weak, sentimental and insipid, originated as a disparaging reference to which poet?
- ⊔ Edmund Spenser
- ⊔ Ambrose Phillips
- ⊔ John Clare

59. *Nausea* was the debut novel of which philosopher?
- ⊔ Bertrand Russell
- ⊔ Ludwig Wittgenstein
- ⊔ Jean-Paul Sartre

60. The Great Dismal Swamp is the name given to a large marshy area in the south-east of which country?
- ⊔ Australia
- ⊔ USA
- ⊔ South Africa

ANSWERS ON P.282

61. Which DJ retired as presenter of the Radio 2 *Breakfast Show* in 2009?
- ⌙ Terry Wogan
- ⌙ Ken Bruce
- ⌙ Johnnie Walker

62. Mount Ossa is the highest point in which Australian state?
- ⌙ Western Australia
- ⌙ Queensland
- ⌙ Tasmania

63. Which Soviet cosmonaut became the first man to step out of a spacecraft and walk in space in 1965?
- ⌙ Alexei Leonov
- ⌙ Leonid Popov
- ⌙ Yuri Romanenko

64. Which creatures belong to the order *Anura*?
- ⌙ Ducks and Geese
- ⌙ Frogs and Toads
- ⌙ Boas and Pythons

65. Who became President of South Africa in May 2009?
- ⌙ Morgan Tsvangirai
- ⌙ Thabo Mbeki
- ⌙ Jacob Zuma

66. In International Morse Code, which letter of the alphabet is represented by a single dot?
- ⌙ A
- ⌙ E
- ⌙ I

ANSWERS ON P.282

67. The national flag of which country consists of a blue cross, outlined in white, on a red background?
- ⊔ Denmark
- ⊔ Finland
- ⊔ Norway

68. The actress Leslie Mann married which film director in 1997?
- ⊔ Judd Apatow
- ⊔ Len Wiseman
- ⊔ Joel Coen

69. 'Nystagmus' refers principally to involuntary movements of which part of the human body?
- ⊔ Feet
- ⊔ Hands
- ⊔ Eyes

70. In which decade did Emerson Fittipaldi win the Formula 1 Driver's World Championship twice?
- ⊔ 1950s
- ⊔ 1960s
- ⊔ 1970s

71. In heraldry, what term is used to describe a lion in a walking position?
- ⊔ Rampant
- ⊔ Passant
- ⊔ Couchant

72. Which US city is home to Columbia University, a member of the Ivy League?
- ⊔ Philadelphia
- ⊔ Detroit
- ⊔ New York

ANSWERS ON P.282

73. The Bayeux Tapestry is made from woollen thread embroidered on a canvas of which textile?
- ⌐ Linen
- ⌐ Silk
- ⌐ Hessian

74. For what does the letter 'I' stand in the medical abbreviation 'ICU'?
- ⌐ Internal
- ⌐ Intensive
- ⌐ Incident

75. Who might use an instrument called a 'maulstick'?
- ⌐ Artist
- ⌐ Bee-keeper
- ⌐ Manicurist

76. The coastal area of which county in Wales was designated a National Park in 1952?
- ⌐ Pembrokeshire
- ⌐ Conwy
- ⌐ Monmouthshire

77. What is the title of Annie Proulx's second novel, which won the Pulitzer Fiction Prize in 1994?
- ⌐ The Shipping News
- ⌐ The Hours
- ⌐ American Pastoral

78. 'Puggaree' is an Indian term for which item of clothing?
- ⌐ Knee-length shirt
- ⌐ Loincloth
- ⌐ Turban

ANSWERS ON P.282

79. The Rose Bruford College in Kent was the first in Britain to offer an Honours Degree in which subject?
- ⎵ Drama
- ⎵ Horticulture
- ⎵ Food Science

80. Walter Sisulu was a prominent activist and politician in which country?
- ⎵ Kenya
- ⎵ South Africa
- ⎵ Zimbabwe

81. What instrument did Dave Clark play in his band the Dave Clark Five?
- ⎵ Keyboard
- ⎵ Bass Guitar
- ⎵ Drums

82. The *Cutty Sark* was built in and launched from which Scottish shipbuilding town in 1869?
- ⎵ Dumbarton
- ⎵ Clydebank
- ⎵ Greenock

83. What name is given to a large boulder so delicately poised on its base that it will rock when pushed?
- ⎵ Logan Stone
- ⎵ Harlow Stone
- ⎵ Brindle Stone

84. Who was the last Roman Catholic Archbishop of Canterbury, fulfilling the role from 1556 to 1558?
- ⎵ Simon Islip
- ⎵ Reginald Pole
- ⎵ Thomas Herring

ANSWERS ON P.282

85. The songs 'Wonderful Copenhagen' and 'Inchworm' come from a film musical about which famous writer?
- ⊔ Edgar Rice Burroughs
- ⊔ Rudyard Kipling
- ⊔ Hans Christian Andersen

86. 'Natation' is a literary word for which activity?
- ⊔ Sleeping
- ⊔ Swimming
- ⊔ Sewing

87. Ophiology is the study of which creatures?
- ⊔ Snakes
- ⊔ Ants
- ⊔ Bats

88. Who was the third President of the United States of America?
- ⊔ James Madison
- ⊔ Thomas Jefferson
- ⊔ John Adams

89. Which historical novelist wrote the 2008 book *Azincourt*?
- ⊔ Bernard Cornwell
- ⊔ Conn Iggulden
- ⊔ Simon Scarrow

90. In 1976, the first scheduled Concorde flights from London flew to which destination?
- ⊔ Dubai
- ⊔ Bahrain
- ⊔ Abu Dhabi

ANSWERS ON P.282

91. 'Stovepipes' is a term for what item of clothing?
 ⊔ Socks
 ⊔ Waistcoats
 ⊔ Trousers

92. Ola Jordan won *Strictly Come Dancing* in 2009 with which celebrity?
 ⊔ Ricky Whittle
 ⊔ Chris Hollins
 ⊔ Phil Tufnell

93. Who launched his own clothing range called Pretty Green in 2009?
 ⊔ Will Young
 ⊔ Robbie Williams
 ⊔ Liam Gallagher

94. DND is the international Air Transport Association code for which city's airport?
 ⊔ Dundee
 ⊔ Dunedin
 ⊔ Dusseldorf

95. What is the name of the country house in Wiltshire that is home to the Marquess of Bath?
 ⊔ Chatsworth
 ⊔ Longleat
 ⊔ Cliveden

96. In classical mythology, a hamadryad is a type of nymph who lives in a what?
 ⊔ Tree
 ⊔ Cave
 ⊔ River

ANSWERS ON P.282

97. What is used to play the game 'euchre'?
- ⊔ Marbles
- ⊔ Cards
- ⊔ Dice

98. Which famous duo had their first meeting at the Midland Hotel in Manchester in 1904?
- ⊔ Watson and Crick
- ⊔ Laurel and Hardy
- ⊔ Rolls and Royce

99. Wolfgang Puck is a leading name in which field?
- ⊔ Art
- ⊔ Cookery
- ⊔ Architecture

100. What name is given to the brownish foam that forms on the top of freshly made espresso coffee?
- ⊔ Crema
- ⊔ Cucina
- ⊔ Corova

ANSWERS ON P.282

PAT GIBSON

FULL NAME:
Patrick Gibson

HOME TOWN:
Born in Galway – I now live in Wigan

EDUCATION:
Degree in Civil Engineering.

QUIZZING CREDENTIALS:

Who Wants to Be a Millionaire?	2004
Mastermind	2005
Brain of Britain	2006
World Quizzing Champion	2007, 2010, 2011 and 2013
Mastermind Champion of Champions	2010
Are You an Egghead? Series 2	2009

STRONGEST *EGGHEADS* SUBJECT:
I decided a long time ago to try to be capable across the full range of general knowledge. Whenever I sense a weaker area I do some work on it.

LEAST FAVOURITE SUBJECT:
I really don't mind what category I'm picked for. It's always interesting to see what comes up and which Egghead the opposing team select for the question room. Each category has its own charms – interesting questions get asked right across the spectrum.

SPECIAL INTEREST / HOBBIES:
I do a lot of work on my quizzing. I swim a lot for enjoyment and fitness.

WHAT DOES IT TAKE TO BE AN EGGHEAD:
Being interested in a wide range of things is a great help. A good memory is obviously a big bonus. I read the papers avidly and take note of interesting snippets. I have done this for years so it's ingrained and automatic by now.

WHO WOULD BE ON YOUR ULTIMATE FANTASY QUIZ TEAM:
This would depend what type of quiz the team was competing in . . . *Eggheads*, table, *University Challenge*-like buzzing etc. I have played many times on the England national team which is pretty strong – that's myself, Kevin, Jesse Honey and Olav Bjortomt.

MOST MEMORABLE MOMENT DURING YOUR TIME AS AN EGGHEAD:
We had a young boy, Adam, come to watch a filming once – though paralysed, he is a very keen fan of the show.

WHAT ADVICE DO YOU HAVE FOR ANY BUDDING EGGHEADS:
Were the path to Egghead-dom through an *Are You an Egghead?* type contest then, alongside knowing as much 'stuff' as you can, a cool head and fighting spirit are essential. As an Egghead, meeting new teams is a great pleasure as is being at the heart of a succession of quiz contests. Every show is different.

WHAT IS YOUR FAVOURITE FACT/ PIECE OF TRIVIA:
This changes all the time – there's so much good stuff. A recent tidbit from the newspaper that caught my eye is the question: 'It's name taken from an Arthur C. Clarke short story, which NASA spacecraft will be launched on a rocket from Cape Canaveral in 2014

and will use a 13,000 sq ft sail to ride the solar winds, orbiting the Sun monitoring solar flares? It will also carry cremated remains of Gene / Majel Roddenberry and James Doohan. Answer: Sunjammer.

LITTLE KNOWN FACT ABOUT YOU:
I played table tennis for my university – a long time ago.

1. Which English city is home to a variety of small passages, alleys and footpaths, collectively known as 'snickelways'?
   ⊔ York
   ⊔ Winchester
   ⊔ Coventry

2. Guyana, in South America, has a coastline on which ocean?
   ⊔ Atlantic
   ⊔ Pacific
   ⊔ Indian

3. The scenic '17-Mile Drive' is a feature of which US state?
   ⊔ Arizona
   ⊔ Wyoming
   ⊔ California

4. Which two colours feature on the Saudi Arabian flag?
   ⊔ Red and Black
   ⊔ Green and White
   ⊔ Blue and Yellow

5. In which country is the active Tungurahua volcano located?
   ⊔ Venezuela
   ⊔ Ecuador
   ⊔ Chile

6. Kandahar is a city and region in which Asian country?
   ⊔ Afghanistan
   ⊔ Bangladesh
   ⊔ Tajikistan

ANSWERS ON P.283

7. Bikini Atoll is located in which ocean?
   ⏄ Atlantic
   ⏄ Indian
   ⏄ Pacific

8. The island of Falster in the Baltic Sea is part of which country?
   ⏄ Estonia
   ⏄ Denmark
   ⏄ Finland

9. California has borders with Arizona, Nevada and which other US state?
   ⏄ Washington
   ⏄ Idaho
   ⏄ Oregon

10. What is the official currency of Luxembourg?
    ⏄ Franc
    ⏄ Pound
    ⏄ Euro

11. The island of Sri Lanka is located in which ocean?
    ⏄ Indian
    ⏄ Atlantic
    ⏄ Pacific

12. The ski resort of Méribel is in which country?
    ⏄ France
    ⏄ Switzerland
    ⏄ Italy

ANSWERS ON P.283

13. What is the largest, but most sparsely populated, South African province?
  ⊔ Limpopo
  ⊔ Northern Cape
  ⊔ Free State

14. The Essequibo, which is over 600 miles in length, is the longest river in which country?
  ⊔ Chile
  ⊔ Paraguay
  ⊔ Guyana

15. Where in England is the junction called Scotch Corner where the A66 meets the A1?
  ⊔ North London
  ⊔ North Yorkshire
  ⊔ Northamptonshire

16. In the UK, the arch of St Brides Bay faces out towards which larger body of water?
  ⊔ Atlantic Ocean
  ⊔ North Sea
  ⊔ English Channel

17. Which term refers to a type of very shallow soil on top of bedrock?
  ⊔ Podzol
  ⊔ Gley
  ⊔ Ranker

18. What name is given to a type of long streamlined rock formation often created by wind erosion and found in deserts?
  ⊔ Geest
  ⊔ Yardang
  ⊔ Yazoo

ANSWERS ON P.283

19. Cape Disappointment is a promontory and a state park in which US state?
- ␣ Maine
- ␣ Florida
- ␣ Washington

20. The Blackwall Tunnel passes under which English river?
- ␣ Trent
- ␣ Thames
- ␣ Tyne

21. In which Asian country is the city of Jodhpur located?
- ␣ India
- ␣ Sri Lanka
- ␣ Afghanistan

22. The towns of Petersfield and Midhurst are located in which national park?
- ␣ South Downs
- ␣ Cairngorms
- ␣ Brecon Beacons

23. What is the capital of the French region of Brittany?
- ␣ Rennes
- ␣ Saint Malo
- ␣ Poitiers

24. Which country shares land borders with Austria, Hungary, Croatia and Italy?
- ␣ Slovakia
- ␣ Serbia
- ␣ Slovenia

ANSWERS ON P.283

25. The Shrine of the Báb is a feature of the port of Haifa in which country?
    ⌐ Egypt
    ⌐ Israel
    ⌐ Libya

26. The Sulu Sea is part of which ocean?
    ⌐ Arctic
    ⌐ Pacific
    ⌐ Atlantic

27. Sumburgh Airport is the main airport serving which island?
    ⌐ Shetland
    ⌐ Guernsey
    ⌐ Isle of Wight

28. Jesmond, Haymarket and Ilford Road are stations on which city's underground railway system?
    ⌐ Newcastle Upon Tyne
    ⌐ Manchester
    ⌐ London

29. Baluchistan is the name of an arid, mountainous region that includes parts of Iran, Pakistan and which other country?
    ⌐ Afghanistan
    ⌐ Tajikistan
    ⌐ Kazakhstan

30. The Pelagie Islands in the Mediterranean Sea are territories of which country?
    ⌐ Italy
    ⌐ France
    ⌐ Greece

ANSWERS ON P.283

31. The Italian port of Brindisi is located on which body of water?

⌴ Adriatic Sea

⌴ Ligurian Sea

⌴ Aegean Sea

32. In square miles, what is the approximate area of Singapore?

⌴ 27

⌴ 274

⌴ 2,740

33. The village of Pluckley, often described as the most haunted village in England, is in which county?

⌴ Hertfordshire

⌴ Norfolk

⌴ Kent

34. Gasherbrum is the name given to a group of peaks in which mountain range?

⌴ Karakorum

⌴ Caucasus

⌴ Taurus

35. The group of islands known as the Recherche Archipelago lies off the coast of which country?

⌴ South Africa

⌴ Australia

⌴ Canada

36. In which country was the province of Flevoland established in 1986?

⌴ Belgium

⌴ Austria

⌴ Netherlands

ANSWERS ON P.283

37. Which state in the United States is divided into parishes rather than counties?
- ⊔ Rhode Island
- ⊔ Louisiana
- ⊔ Minnesota

38. Wiesbaden is the capital of which German state?
- ⊔ Saarland
- ⊔ Hesse
- ⊔ Brandenburg

39. Which island lies directly north of Sardinia?
- ⊔ Corsica
- ⊔ Corfu
- ⊔ Crete

40. What type of geographical feature is Nanga Parbat in Pakistan?
- ⊔ Forest
- ⊔ Mountain
- ⊔ Lake

41. The French city of Nantes stands on the estuary of which river?
- ⊔ Rhône
- ⊔ Loire
- ⊔ Seine

42. What is the largest city, in terms of population, on the South Island of New Zealand?
- ⊔ Christchurch
- ⊔ Dunedin
- ⊔ Hamilton

ANSWERS ON P.283

43. The Lake District is in which county?
- ⌙ North Yorkshire
- ⌙ Derbyshire
- ⌙ Cumbria

44. Which Asian capital city is situated on the island of Luzon?
- ⌙ Manila
- ⌙ Tokyo
- ⌙ Seoul

45. The Kara Sea is part of which ocean?
- ⌙ Arctic
- ⌙ Pacific
- ⌙ Atlantic

46. How many stars appear on the flag of Honduras?
- ⌙ 1
- ⌙ 3
- ⌙ 5

47. Which seaside resort is located at the northern end of a nature reserve called Gibraltar Point?
- ⌙ Blackpool
- ⌙ Skegness
- ⌙ Great Yarmouth

48. Which term refers to a hillside or mountain slope that receives little sunshine?
- ⌙ Umland
- ⌙ Ultisol
- ⌙ Ubac

ANSWERS ON P.283

49. Tripoli, the capital of Libya, is located on which body of water?
- ⮡ Red Sea
- ⮡ Gulf of Aden
- ⮡ Mediterranean Sea

50. What is the monetary unit of Belize?
- ⮡ Belize Peso
- ⮡ Belize Pound
- ⮡ Belize Dollar

51. The Wolverine State is a nickname of which US state?
- ⮡ Minnesota
- ⮡ Michigan
- ⮡ Massachusetts

52. The Lyke Wake Walk from Osmotherley to Ravenscar crosses which National Park?
- ⮡ North York Moors
- ⮡ Snowdonia
- ⮡ New Forest

53. The Bernese Oberland is a section of the Alps that is located in which country?
- ⮡ Germany
- ⮡ Switzerland
- ⮡ Italy

54. Theydon Bois is a village in which English county?
- ⮡ Surrey
- ⮡ Wiltshire
- ⮡ Essex

ANSWERS ON P.283

55. The wide coastal inlet known as the Canterbury Bight is in which ocean?
   ⌐ Pacific
   ⌐ Indian
   ⌐ Arctic

56. Which mountain range rises just east of Adelaide in South Australia?
   ⌐ Great Dividing Range
   ⌐ Ophthalmia Range
   ⌐ Mount Lofty Ranges

57. King Shaka International Airport is the primary airport for which African city?
   ⌐ Durban
   ⌐ Nairobi
   ⌐ Casablanca

58. What is the name of the headland near Selsey in West Sussex?
   ⌐ Selsey Bill
   ⌐ Selsey Tom
   ⌐ Selsey Jack

59. Saint Bartholomew's Cathedral and the birthplace of Goethe are features of which German city?
   ⌐ Frankfurt
   ⌐ Cologne
   ⌐ Munich

60. Palawan and Basilan are islands of which country?
   ⌐ Indonesia
   ⌐ Philippines
   ⌐ Malaysia

ANSWERS ON P.283

61. Which Scottish town has a name which translates as 'loch in
a damp hollow'?
⊔ Aviemore
⊔ Invergarry
⊔ Linlithgow

62. Pikes Peak is a mountain in which North American range?
⊔ Ozarks
⊔ Rockies
⊔ Catskills

63. The three-fingered peninsula called Halkidiki is in which
country?
⊔ Turkey
⊔ Greece
⊔ Israel

64. The horizontal stripes on the flag of India are orange, white
and which other colour?
⊔ Black
⊔ Red
⊔ Green

65. The Yangtze river is approximately how many miles long?
⊔ 4,000 miles
⊔ 14,000 miles
⊔ 40,000 miles

66. Which French city is the capital of the Bouches-du-Rhône
département in southern France?
⊔ Marseille
⊔ Nice
⊔ Perpignan

ANSWERS ON P.283

67. Lourenço Marques is the former name of which African capital city?

- Maputo
- Luanda
- Freetown

68. What is the official monetary unit of Belgium?

- Euro
- Franc
- Pound

69. What is the approximate population of the UK?

- 42 Million
- 52 Million
- 62 Million

70. Kingsford Smith Airport is located in which city?

- Adelaide
- Sydney
- Perth

71. How high, in metres, is Cross Fell, the highest point in the Pennines?

- 493
- 693
- 893

72. The east coast of Saudi Arabia is bordered by which body of water?

- Red Sea
- Arabian Sea
- Persian Gulf

ANSWERS ON P.283

73. The town of Bakewell, home of the Bakewell Pudding, is located in which national park?
- North York Moors
- Lake District
- Peak District

74. Which two colours feature on the flag of Albania?
- Black and Red
- Blue and Yellow
- Green and White

75. For what does the word 'ciudad' usually stand in Spanish or South American place names?
- City
- Hill
- Sea

76. How many countries border the Black Sea?
- 3
- 6
- 9

77. Which lake in central Switzerland has the German name Vierwaldstättersee, or 'Lake of the Four Forested Cantons'?
- Lake Geneva
- Lake Lucerne
- Lake Constance

78. The Gulf of Carpentaria is enclosed on three sides by which country?
- Canada
- Mexico
- Australia

ANSWERS ON P.283

79. Luanda, the capital of Angola, is a port on which ocean?
- ⊔ Pacific
- ⊔ Atlantic
- ⊔ Indian

80. What name is given to a cylindrical mass of solidified lava formed in the vent of a volcano?
- ⊔ Cork
- ⊔ Spigot
- ⊔ Plug

81. The River Otter flows through Somerset and which other English county?
- ⊔ Devon
- ⊔ Dorset
- ⊔ Wiltshire

82. Lake Winnipeg drains into Hudson Bay via which river?
- ⊔ Nelson River
- ⊔ Wellington River
- ⊔ Montgomery River

83. Panaji, also called Panjim, is the capital of which western Indian state?
- ⊔ Kerala
- ⊔ Orissa
- ⊔ Goa

84. Which desert covers parts of several countries including Egypt, Libya and Tunisia?
- ⊔ Gobi
- ⊔ Kalahari
- ⊔ Sahara

ANSWERS ON P.283

85. Marmolada is the highest peak in which mountain range?
- ☐ Pyrenees
- ☐ Apennines
- ☐ Dolomites

86. Ashdown Forest, the inspiration for A.A. Milne's *Winnie the Pooh* stories, is located in which county?
- ☐ Dorset
- ☐ Gloucestershire
- ☐ East Sussex

87. What is the approximate population of Mongolia?
- ☐ 3 Million
- ☐ 13 Million
- ☐ 23 Million

88. In terms of population, what is the largest city in Wales?
- ☐ Cardiff
- ☐ Swansea
- ☐ Newport

89. What was the currency of the Netherlands before the introduction of the Euro?
- ☐ Krone
- ☐ Markka
- ☐ Guilder

90. The resort of Fuengirola is located on which of the Spanish Costas?
- ☐ Costa Brava
- ☐ Costa Blanca
- ☐ Costa del Sol

ANSWERS ON P.283

91. Traditionally, Canada's Prairie Provinces are Alberta, Manitoba and which other?
- Saskatchewan
- New Brunswick
- Prince Edward Island

92. The cities of Palembang in Indonesia, Udaipur in India and Osaka in Japan all share which nickname?
- London of the East
- Venice of the East
- Paris of the East

93. Sotonian is a term for a person from which English city?
- Sunderland
- Southampton
- Stoke-on-Trent

94. The town of Cleveleys is located approximately four miles north of which seaside resort?
- Great Yarmouth
- Hastings
- Blackpool

95. What is the approximate population of Sweden?
- 9 Million
- 19 Million
- 29 Million

96. Mount Kosciuszko, the highest peak in Australia, is located in which major mountain range?
- West Coast Range
- Great Dividing Range
- Napier Range

ANSWERS ON P.283

97. What is the capital of the South African province of
Gauteng?
⊔ Bloemfontein
⊔ Johannesburg
⊔ Durban

98. Studland Bay is a feature of which English county?
⊔ Kent
⊔ Dorset
⊔ Norfolk

99. What is the capital of the United Arab Emirates?
⊔ Shiraz
⊔ Fujairah
⊔ Abu Dhabi

100. The island of Formentera lies due south of which of the
Balearic Islands?
⊔ Minorca
⊔ Majorca
⊔ Ibiza

ANSWERS ON P.283

1. Which French term refers to the basic position or stance in fencing?
   - ⊔ En Garde
   - ⊔ A Propos
   - ⊔ A Point

2. Mold is an administrative centre of an area in which part of the UK?
   - ⊔ Scotland
   - ⊔ England
   - ⊔ Wales

3. 'Can Queen Victoria Eat Cold Apple Pie' is a mnemonic for remembering what?
   - ⊔ Labours of Heracles
   - ⊔ Pharaohs of Egypt
   - ⊔ Hills of Rome

4. What are the main ingredients of the French dish 'aligot'?
   - ⊔ Mashed Potato and Cheese
   - ⊔ Baked Apples and Sultanas
   - ⊔ Braised Beef and Mushrooms

5. What type of creature is the kune kune from New Zealand?
   - ⊔ Snake
   - ⊔ Pig
   - ⊔ Duck

6. What term is used to refer to a legal document that amends a previously existing will?
   - ⊔ Bequest
   - ⊔ Probate
   - ⊔ Codicil

ANSWERS ON P.284

7. What name is given to the public announcements in a parish church that a marriage is going to take place between two specified persons?
   - ⌐ Banns
   - ⌐ Hunns
   - ⌐ Minns

8. What name is given to the dish of baked beans with salt pork and treacle added?
   - ⌐ Baltimore Baked Beans
   - ⌐ Boise Baked Beans
   - ⌐ Boston Baked Beans

9. Which TV presenter and food expert was a member of a punk band called Jet Bronx and the Forbidden?
   - ⌐ Loyd Grossman
   - ⌐ Gordon Ramsay
   - ⌐ Delia Smith

10. For which Australian state cricket side did Ian Botham play between 1987 and 1988?
    - ⌐ New South Wales
    - ⌐ Tasmania
    - ⌐ Queensland

11. Mausolus, for whom the Mausoleum at Halicarnassus was built, was a ruler of which region?
    - ⌐ Pontus
    - ⌐ Caria
    - ⌐ Galatia

12. Sasquatch is an alternative name for which mythical creature?
    - ⌐ Barghest
    - ⌐ Bigfoot
    - ⌐ Loch Ness Monster

ANSWERS ON P.284

13. What term is used to refer to an uncastrated male horse?
- ⊔ Stallion
- ⊔ Gelding
- ⊔ Steer

14. 'Frühling' is the German word for which season?
- ⊔ Spring
- ⊔ Summer
- ⊔ Autumn

15. Lisa Kudrow, best known for her role as Phoebe in *Friends*, played a waitress called Ursula Buffay in which sitcom?
- ⊔ Mad About You
- ⊔ Frasier
- ⊔ Taxi

16. 'Mourning cloak' is the American name for which butterfly?
- ⊔ Red Admiral
- ⊔ Cabbage White
- ⊔ Camberwell Beauty

17. The term 'genial' can be used in relation to which part of the body?
- ⊔ Bridge of the Nose
- ⊔ Belly Button
- ⊔ Chin

18. The Hall of Mirrors, designed by Mansart in the 1670s, is a famous feature of which royal palace?
- ⊔ Buckingham Palace
- ⊔ Winter Palace, St Petersburg
- ⊔ Palace of Versailles

ANSWERS ON P.284

19. What colour is cyan?
  ⌂ Greenish-blue
  ⌂ Reddish-brown
  ⌂ Pinkish-red

20. Which major Christian feast, which falls on the 15th of August, is a public holiday in many countries?
  ⌂ Epiphany
  ⌂ Corpus Christi
  ⌂ Assumption

21. Dating from before World War II, what is a Susie-Q?
  ⌂ Coat
  ⌂ Dance Step
  ⌂ Hairstyle

22. *Le Beau Serge* and *The Cousins* are films directed by which French film maker?
  ⌂ François Truffaut
  ⌂ Jean-Luc Godard
  ⌂ Claude Chabrol

23. The *Nyctaginaceae* family of flowering plants, which includes the bougainvillea, is also known by what name?
  ⌂ Sunrise Family
  ⌂ Four-O'Clock Family
  ⌂ Midnight Family

24. 'Strine' is a version of English said to be spoken by people from which country?
  ⌂ USA
  ⌂ South Africa
  ⌂ Australia

ANSWERS ON P.284

25. Someone referred to as 'pulchritudinous' can also be described by which term?
- ⌣ Beautiful
- ⌣ Smelly
- ⌣ Arrogant

26. Which item of furniture is an 'armoire'?
- ⌣ Chest of Drawers
- ⌣ Wardrobe
- ⌣ Table

27. A modern style of which common foodstuff was developed in the 1720s by a Mrs Clements of Durham?
- ⌣ Ketchup
- ⌣ Worcestershire Sauce
- ⌣ Mustard

28. What name did David Cameron give to his baby, born in August 2010?
- ⌣ Paris
- ⌣ Florence
- ⌣ London

29. What type of meat is usually served at a traditional Thanksgiving dinner?
- ⌣ Turkey
- ⌣ Rabbit
- ⌣ Lamb

30. Which cocktail was invented at the famous Raffles Hotel?
- ⌣ Singapore Sling
- ⌣ Mojito
- ⌣ Bellini

ANSWERS ON P.284

31. Who became manager of Aston Villa FC in September 2010?
- ⊔ Claudio Ranieri
- ⊔ José Mourinho
- ⊔ Gérard Houllier

32. Which London Underground line serves the terminals of Heathrow Airport?
- ⊔ Piccadilly
- ⊔ Metropolitan
- ⊔ Bakerloo

33. In 2003, a college at Durham University was re-named in honour of which actor?
- ⊔ Alec Guinness
- ⊔ John Mills
- ⊔ Peter Ustinov

34. What was the middle name of the Greek shipping magnate Aristotle Onassis?
- ⊔ Socrates
- ⊔ Plato
- ⊔ Diogenes

35. The Yenisei River empties into which ocean?
- ⊔ Atlantic
- ⊔ Arctic
- ⊔ Indian

36. With only 21 verses, which is the shortest book of the Old Testament?
- ⊔ Micah
- ⊔ Obadiah
- ⊔ Isaiah

ANSWERS ON P.284

37. The Latin phrase 'cave canem' means 'beware of the ...' what?
- ⌐ Dog
- ⌐ Low Ceiling
- ⌐ Potholes

38. What is the name of the band who won the 2010 Mercury Music Prize?
- ⌐ The xx
- ⌐ The yy
- ⌐ The zz

39. Under whose premiership was the 'Citizen's Charter' launched?
- ⌐ Margaret Thatcher
- ⌐ John Major
- ⌐ Tony Blair

40. In 2009, whom did Vincent Nichols succeed as Archbishop of Westminster?
- ⌐ Basil Hume
- ⌐ William Godfrey
- ⌐ Cormac Murphy-O'Connor

41. Russell Kane and Russell Howard are well known names in which field?
- ⌐ Photography
- ⌐ Cookery
- ⌐ Comedy

42. What nickname was often given to Henry Ford's Model T car?
- ⌐ T-Rex
- ⌐ Tin Lizzie
- ⌐ Think Tank

ANSWERS ON P.284

43. Who once described the House of Lords as 'the British Outer Mongolia for retired politicians'?
    ⌴ Tony Benn
    ⌴ Ken Livingstone
    ⌴ Alan Sugar

44. The Unesco World Heritage site known as the Gondwana Rainforests are located in which country?
    ⌴ India
    ⌴ Australia
    ⌴ Japan

45. Goodluck Jonathan was sworn in as the new president of which country in May 2010?
    ⌴ Nigeria
    ⌴ Angola
    ⌴ Ethiopia

46. Events surrounding which legendary figure are said to have caused the Trojan War?
    ⌴ Messalina
    ⌴ Cleopatra
    ⌴ Helen

47. Giles Coren and Jay Rayner found fame as critics of what?
    ⌴ Computer Games
    ⌴ Music
    ⌴ Restaurants

48. Which Cardinal was beatified at a Mass held in Birmingham during the Pope's visit to Britain in 2010?
    ⌴ John Henry Newman
    ⌴ Basil Hume
    ⌴ Reginald Pole

ANSWERS ON P.284

49. In which country is Amharic one of the main languages?
- ⊔ Suriname
- ⊔ Papua New Guinea
- ⊔ Ethiopia

50. A statue to Tommy Cooper, erected in 2008 in his home town of Caerphilly, was unveiled by which actor?
- ⊔ Anthony Hopkins
- ⊔ Ioan Gruffudd
- ⊔ Jonathan Pryce

51. What nickname was given to the public bicycles that were placed on London streets in 2010?
- ⊔ Bendy Bikes
- ⊔ Boris Bikes
- ⊔ Bloomsbury Bikes

52. Between 1975 and 1979, who played the title role in the US TV series *Wonder Woman*?
- ⊔ Farrah Fawcett
- ⊔ Angie Dickinson
- ⊔ Lynda Carter

53. Manuka honey, which is known for its antibacterial and healing benefits, is produced in which country?
- ⊔ Namibia
- ⊔ New Zealand
- ⊔ Nicaragua

54. What type of food are the French 'Boules de Berlin'?
- ⊔ Onion Rings
- ⊔ Doughnuts
- ⊔ Dumplings

ANSWERS ON P.284

55. In 1993, Simon Hoggart became a parliamentary sketch writer for which daily newspaper?
- Daily Mail
- The Guardian
- The Times

56. Where on a ship is the prow located?
- At the Front
- In the Middle
- At the Back

57. What name is given to fabric woven with a pattern of diagonal parallel ribs?
- Twipp
- Twirt
- Twill

58. Which duo featured on the Royal Mail's 2010 Christmas stamps?
- Wallace and Gromit
- Prince William and Prince Harry
- The Two Ronnies

59. During World War II, which section of the German armed forces, or Wehrmacht, was known as the 'Heer'?
- Army
- Navy
- Air Force

60. Originating in the Canary Islands, what is a 'timple'?
- Semicircular Plate
- Stringed Instrument
- Tassel-covered Dress

ANSWERS ON P.284

61. The American football linebacker Dick Butkus played for which team from 1965 to 1973?
- ⊔ Minnesota Vikings
- ⊔ Dallas Cowboys
- ⊔ Chicago Bears

62. 'Six of One' is a fan club dedicated to which cult TV series?
- ⊔ The Prisoner
- ⊔ Star Trek
- ⊔ Blake's 7

63. If you ordered 'huîtres' in a French restaurant, what type of seafood would you expect to be served?
- ⊔ Shrimps
- ⊔ Mussels
- ⊔ Oysters

64. Which detective was introduced in the novel *Knots and Crosses*?
- ⊔ Rebus
- ⊔ Poirot
- ⊔ Wexford

65. What name was given to the influential people who gathered at the home of Nancy Astor in the 1930s?
- ⊔ Blenheim Circle
- ⊔ Woburn Group
- ⊔ Cliveden Set

66. Which grape variety is thought to take its name from a French word meaning 'young blackbird'?
- ⊔ Pinotage
- ⊔ Merlot
- ⊔ Gamay

ANSWERS ON P.284

67. In 2010, Karren Brady became vice-chairman of which football club?
- ⌿ Blackburn Rovers
- ⌿ Everton
- ⌿ West Ham United

68. The Irish name Seamus is the equivalent of which English name?
- ⌿ John
- ⌿ Jerome
- ⌿ James

69. What type of craftsman is most associated with 'Flemish Bond' and 'English Bond'?
- ⌿ Tiler
- ⌿ Glazier
- ⌿ Bricklayer

70. In Greek mythology, who cleaned the Augean Stables?
- ⌿ Heracles
- ⌿ Jason
- ⌿ Theseus

71. The Potala Palace is the former home of which spiritual leader?
- ⌿ Dalai Lama
- ⌿ Pope
- ⌿ Aga Khan

72. Which American humourist was the author of *The Devil's Dictionary*?
- ⌿ Robert Benchley
- ⌿ Ambrose Bierce
- ⌿ Mark Twain

ANSWERS ON P.284

73. In Greek mythology, Nyx, the female personification of night, was the daughter of whom?
- ⊔ Nemesis
- ⊔ Chaos
- ⊔ Pandemonium

74. The International Airport at Tirana in Albania is named after which famous person?
- ⊔ Enver Hoxha
- ⊔ Mother Teresa
- ⊔ Kemal Atatürk

75. In which country was the cheese 'Oka' first made by Trappist monks over a hundred years ago?
- ⊔ Canada
- ⊔ Spain
- ⊔ New Zealand

76. What name is given to the Iron Age earthwork, which stretches across part of southern Ulster?
- ⊔ Black Pig's Dyke
- ⊔ Brown Cow's Mound
- ⊔ White Horse Hill

77. Sebastián Piñera became president of which South American country in 2010?
- ⊔ Brazil
- ⊔ Argentina
- ⊔ Chile

78. What normally powers the mode of transport known as a 'landau'?
- ⊔ Steam
- ⊔ Magnets
- ⊔ Horses

ANSWERS ON P.284

79. Rosemary Shrager is a well-known name in which field?
- ⎵ Fashion
- ⎵ Dance
- ⎵ Cookery

80. Which Oscar-winning actor was one of the original producers of the stage musical *We Will Rock You*?
- ⎵ Sean Penn
- ⎵ Robert De Niro
- ⎵ Russell Crowe

81. Which French writer disappeared in a plane crash in the Mediterranean in 1944?
- ⎵ Antoine de Saint-Exupéry
- ⎵ Marcel Proust
- ⎵ Albert Camus

82. What type of plant is the Joshua tree?
- ⎵ Palm
- ⎵ Cactus
- ⎵ Yucca

83. Jalfrezi is a type of which foodstuff?
- ⎵ Cheese
- ⎵ Cabbage
- ⎵ Curry

84. Ralph Lauren is a famous name in which field?
- ⎵ Dance
- ⎵ Fashion
- ⎵ Science

ANSWERS ON P.284

85. In which South American country were miners trapped underground for more than two months in 2010?
- ⌣ Peru
- ⌣ Brazil
- ⌣ Chile

86. 'The rest is silence' is the last line spoken by which Shakespeare character?
- ⌣ Hamlet
- ⌣ Macbeth
- ⌣ Romeo

87. The Haflinger is a South Tyrolean breed of which creature?
- ⌣ Goat
- ⌣ Horse
- ⌣ Cow

88. Soul singer Cee Lo Green, who had a UK number one single in 2010 with 'Forget You', was a member of which pop duo?
- ⌣ Massive Attack
- ⌣ Gnarls Barkley
- ⌣ Röyksopp

89. At which football tournament was the England team involved in the notorious 'Dentist's Chair' celebration?
- ⌣ Italia 90
- ⌣ USA 94
- ⌣ Euro 96

90. In the USA, G-Man is a term particularly used to describe employees of which organisation?
- ⌣ IRS
- ⌣ CIA
- ⌣ FBI

ANSWERS ON P.284

91. A snickersnee is an archaic term for a type of what?
- ⊔ Knife
- ⊔ Pitchfork
- ⊔ Tankard

92. How is the letter A expressed in Morse Code?
- ⊔ Dot Dash
- ⊔ Dot Dot
- ⊔ Dot Dot Dash

93. The French recipe Hachis Parmentier is most similar to which traditional English dish?
- ⊔ Lancashire Hotpot
- ⊔ Steak and Kidney Pudding
- ⊔ Shepherd's Pie

94. Who did Margaret Thatcher succeed as leader of the Conservative Party in 1975?
- ⊔ William Whitelaw
- ⊔ Jim Prior
- ⊔ Edward Heath

95. What type of flowers are particularly associated with Dame Edna Everage?
- ⊔ Gladioli
- ⊔ Chrysanthemums
- ⊔ Tulips

96. What is the technical name of the colour of the Golden Gate Bridge?
- ⊔ American Blue
- ⊔ International Orange
- ⊔ National Grey

ANSWERS ON P.284

97. Walter Frederick Morrison, who died in 2010 aged ninety, is credited with inventing which popular toy?
- ⌴ Yo-yo
- ⌴ Space Hopper
- ⌴ Frisbee

98. Belgian Kriek beer is flavoured with which fruit?
- ⌴ Apple
- ⌴ Peach
- ⌴ Cherry

99. Ruy Lopez is the name of one of the most popular openings in which game?
- ⌴ Snooker
- ⌴ Chess
- ⌴ Contract Bridge

100. Rocha is a variety of which fruit?
- ⌴ Orange
- ⌴ Pear
- ⌴ Apple

ANSWERS ON P.284

KILLER QUESTIONS

These Killer Questions will really test your quizzing mettle. They are a selection of multiple choice and sudden death questions which the Eggheads faced in the final general knowledge round of the programme.

In each case the Eggheads answered incorrectly and lost the game.

How will you do?

1. In 1811, the explorer David Thompson is believed by many to have discovered the first recorded footprints of which legendary creature?
   ⊔ Loch Ness Monster
   ⊔ Yeti
   ⊔ Big Foot

2. At the end of 2006, how many of the USA's 50 states still officially sanctioned the death penalty?
   ⊔ 38
   ⊔ 18
   ⊔ 8

3. Which actor made headlines in November 2006 when he appeared to be drunk on the US chat show *The View*?
   ⊔ Brad Pitt
   ⊔ Jeff Goldblum
   ⊔ Danny DeVito

4. The 18th of February 2007 marked the beginning of which year in the Chinese calendar?
   ⊔ The Pig
   ⊔ The Dog
   ⊔ The Rat

5. From which Pacific nation are the stations Radio Happy Isles and Radio Happy Lagoon broadcast?
   ⊔ Samoa
   ⊔ Papua New Guinea
   ⊔ Solomon Islands

6. Which coin was officially withdrawn from UK circulation in 1993?
   ⊔ Half-crown
   ⊔ Halfpenny
   ⊔ Florin

7. The singer Edith Piaf was famous for her romantic association with which sportsman?
   ⊔ Marcel Cerdan
   ⊔ René Lacoste
   ⊔ Just Fontaine

8. Which Welsh band released the album *Hey Venus!* in August 2007?
   ⊔ Manic Street Preachers
   ⊔ Super Furry Animals
   ⊔ Stereophonics

9. 'The best lack all conviction, while the worst are full of passionate intensity' is a quotation from a poem by which writer?
   ⊔ T.S. Eliot
   ⊔ W.B. Yeats
   ⊔ H.G. Wells

10. During Bill and Hilary Clinton's visit to London in 1997, Tony and Cherie Blair chose to take them to which restaurant instead of holding a formal banquet?
   ⊔ Le Pont De La Tour
   ⊔ The Ivy
   ⊔ The River Café

11. What is the skateboarding term for riding backwards?
   ⊔ Goofy Foot
   ⊔ Fakie
   ⊔ McTwist

12. Cormac McCarthy's novel *No Country for Old Men* takes its title from a poem by which author?
   ⊔ T.S. Eliot
   ⊔ W.B. Yeats
   ⊔ W.H. Auden

ANSWERS ON P.285

13. What is the diameter of the individual clock faces on London's Big Ben?
    ⎵ 3 metres
    ⎵ 7 metres
    ⎵ 11 metres

14. The trio of supermodel friends that became known in high-society as the Trinity was Naomi Campbell, Linda Evangelista and who?
    ⎵ Elle McPherson
    ⎵ Claudia Schiffer
    ⎵ Christy Turlington

15. The 'Venus flytrap' plant is native to which continent?
    ⎵ North America
    ⎵ Australia
    ⎵ Africa

16. The phrase 'belling the cat' referring to the pointlessness of suggesting impractical solutions to problems is inspired by a work of which writer?
    ⎵ Aesop
    ⎵ Chaucer
    ⎵ Voltaire

17. Originating in Korea in the Middle Ages, what is 'Five-Field Kono'?
    ⎵ Martial Art
    ⎵ Board Game
    ⎵ Sequence Dance

18. *Pygmalion* by George Bernard Shaw was first staged in 1913 not in London but in which city?
    ⎵ Chichester
    ⎵ Vienna
    ⎵ Cairo

ANSWERS ON P.285

19. Which familiar word is derived from a legal term in the late Middle Ages for someone who took bribes from both sides?
    - ⌴ Binocular
    - ⌴ Ambidextrous
    - ⌴ Duplicate

20. In the Marvel comic series 'Fantastic Four', what is the superhero alter-ego of Reed Richards?
    - ⌴ The Human Torch
    - ⌴ Mr Fantastic
    - ⌴ The Thing

21. Who was the Liberal Democrat nominee for the 2008 London Mayoral Election?
    - ⌴ Brian Paddick
    - ⌴ Vince Cable
    - ⌴ Chris Huhne

22. The Spring Bank Holiday in the UK is now always held on which day?
    - ⌴ First Monday in May
    - ⌴ Last Monday in May
    - ⌴ Whit Monday

23. When talking about hair and hairstyles, what is an American referring to if he or she mentions 'bangs'?
    - ⌴ Ponytail
    - ⌴ Fringe
    - ⌴ Plaits

24. A 'sit-up-and-beg' is an old-fashioned type of what device?
    - ⌴ Bicycle
    - ⌴ Washing Machine
    - ⌴ Telephone

ANSWERS ON P.285

25. Which artist best known for his black and white scribbly ink drawings started to produce cartoons for the *Guardian* in 2005?
- ⌴ Andy Riley
- ⌴ Mick Bunnage
- ⌴ David Shrigley

26. Sansad is the name of the Parliament of which country?
- ⌴ Sri Lanka
- ⌴ Pakistan
- ⌴ India

27. Lucetta Templeman, also known as Lucette de Sueur, is a character in which 19th-century novel?
- ⌴ Jane Eyre
- ⌴ The Mayor of Casterbridge
- ⌴ Great Expectations

28. In certain African cultures, what is an 'imbongi'?
- ⌴ Doctor
- ⌴ Poet
- ⌴ Priest

29. What type of creature is a sarcastic fringehead?
- ⌴ Bird
- ⌴ Fish
- ⌴ Monkey

30. The Waikato River, the longest river in New Zealand, enters the Tasman Sea at a point just south of which city?
- ⌴ Auckland
- ⌴ Christchurch
- ⌴ Wellington

ANSWERS ON P.285

31. In Japanese cuisine, what are 'Udons'?
- ⌴ Fried Prawns
- ⌴ Thick Noodles
- ⌴ Steamed Dumplings

32. What are the main ingredients of the French dish 'aligot'?
- ⌴ Mashed Potato and Cheese
- ⌴ Baked Apples and Sultanas
- ⌴ Braised Beef and Mushrooms

33. 'Boss' Mangan is a character in which George Bernard Shaw play?
- ⌴ Major Barbara
- ⌴ Heartbreak House
- ⌴ Man and Superman

34. What is the title of the 2010 sequel to Scott Turow's 1987 novel *Presumed Innocent*?
- ⌴ The Confession
- ⌴ Presumed Guilty
- ⌴ Innocent

35. In 2011, magician Paul Daniels was reportedly hit in the head by a pizza thrown at him by which puppet?
- ⌴ Sooty
- ⌴ Basil Brush
- ⌴ Miss Piggy

36. The 'Festa del Redentore', which was first held in 1577 to celebrate the end of a terrible plague, is held in which Italian city?
- ⌴ Rome
- ⌴ Venice
- ⌴ Florence

ANSWERS ON P.285

37. The author who wrote historical thrillers under the name
Ariana Franklin was married to which TV personality?
   ⊔ David Dimbleby
   ⊔ Barry Norman
   ⊔ Michael Aspel

38. In international maritime signalling, which letter of the
alphabet is represented by the Blue Peter flag?
   ⊔ D
   ⊔ P
   ⊔ B

39. 'One must eat to live, and not live to eat' is a quotation from
a play by which writer?
   ⊔ Molière
   ⊔ Brecht
   ⊔ Chekhov

40. Which letter of the alphabet is used to designate the most
powerful type of solar flare?
   ⊔ X
   ⊔ Y
   ⊔ Z

41. Which actress is portrayed by Judi Dench in the 2011 film
My Week with Marilyn?
   ⊔ Sybil Thorndike
   ⊔ Peggy Ashcroft
   ⊔ Cicely Courtneidge

42. What became the flagship of the Royal Navy fleet in 2011?
   ⊔ HMS Bulwark
   ⊔ HMS Argyll
   ⊔ HMS Clyde

ANSWERS ON P.285

43. The Baiyoke Tower II, one of the world's tallest hotels, is located in which Asian country?
- ⊔ Thailand
- ⊔ Sri Lanka
- ⊔ Malaysia

44. What type of vehicle is the 'ship' in the title of the Shirley Temple song 'On The Good Ship Lollipop'?
- ⊔ Plane
- ⊔ Balloon
- ⊔ Submarine

45. 'Good Times' and 'Green Light' were UK number one singles for which group in 2010?

46. Who played Henry Higgins opposite Kara Tointon's Eliza when the 2011 West End production of *Pygmalion* opened?

47. In 1976, the first Winter Paralympics took place in which country?

48. Which Italian fashion designer, famous for his flamboyant, sculptural creations and dubbed by *Women's Wear Daily* as 'The Frank Lloyd Wright of Italian fashion', died in June 2007?

49. Which economist and social reformer wrote the 1944 report 'Full Employment in a Free Society'?

50. To which football club did Diego Maradona return in 1995, having first played for them in the 1980s?

51. The NEFA or North-East Frontier Agency was until 1972 one of the political divisions of which country?

52. The footballer Peter Crouch married which model in 2011?

ANSWERS ON P.285

53. In 2005, the use of the terms 'spinster' and 'bachelor' on UK marriage certificates was discontinued in favour of which word?

54. In March 2009, Mauricio Funes was elected President of which country?

55. Which London building's mosaics are the result of Queen Victoria's complaint that its interior was 'most dreary, dingy and undevotional'?

56. Chesney Hawkes came to fame when he played the title character in which early 1990s film, that also starred Roger Daltrey?

57. Who is credited with the invention of Radio 4's long-running game show *Just a Minute*?

58. Who was the British prime minister at the time when Inheritance Tax replaced Capital Transfer Tax?

59. To which modern-day country is the clove tree believed to be indigenous?

60. The architect I.M. Pei, whose designs include the Louvre Pyramid in Paris, was born in which country?

61. Which football club has the motto 'Victoria Concordia Crescit' which translates as 'victory grows out of harmony'?

62. Which Hindu god is often portrayed as the Lord of the Dance?

63. What term is normally given to the 'heads' side of a coin or medal bearing the image of a ruler or monarch?

64. Which TV quiz host was the subject of a popular urban myth that he played the saxophone solo in the Gerry Rafferty UK hit single 'Baker Street'?

ANSWERS ON P.285

65. Which stage musical first performed in 2005 features the songs 'Electricity' and 'Expressing Yourself'?

66. What was the profession of Luke Hansard after whom the official parliamentary proceedings is named?

67. Which word in the English language is derived from the Latin for 'that which is to be done'.

68. The word 'Shampoo' is derived from which language?

69. Grimsetter is the former name of the airport which serves which British group of Islands?

70. Which fictitious creature was invented by the US cartoonist Al Capp in 1948 and was represented as small, round and ready to fulfil any material need?

71. Which stiff fabric, historically used to line garments, takes its name from the Italian for 'horsehair' and 'linen'?

72. What was the name of the London-based magazine reviewing popular arts and culture that was founded by Julie Burchill, Cosmo Landesman and Toby Young in 1991?

73. *Quod Anglicana ecclesia libera sit*, or 'That the English Church shall be free', is contained in the first clause of which famous document?

74. Which game, particularly popular in the north-east of England, is played by throwing a circular disc with a roughly four-inch hole in the centre over a pin known as a hob?

75. The Cobalt Silver Rush and the Porcupine Gold Rush took place in which country in the early part of the 20th century?

ANSWERS ON P.285

MUSIC

1. The Tweets
2. Mars
3. Edward German
4. Neil Sedaka
5. Cartoon Music
6. Beethoven
7. Chord
8. Tweeter
9. The Who
10. Clarinet
11. Pit
12. Film Scores
13. Raves
14. Sun
15. Paris
16. JLS
17. Al Jarreau
18. Patsy Cline
19. 1970s
20. Violin
21. Cabaret
22. Talking Heads
23. The Banana Boat Song
24. The Kinks
25. Suggs
26. Gretl
27. Chanter
28. Morrissey
29. HMS Pinafore
30. My Way
31. Cats
32. Fun Boy Three
33. Led Zeppelin
34. Chichester
35. Galileo
36. Norwegian Wood
37. Prince
38. Kiss
39. Percussion
40. Elijah Wood
41. Eartha Kitt
42. Norway
43. Consider Yourself
44. 1975
45. Happy Mondays
46. Pomp and Circumstance
47. French
48. Barbershop
49. Cheek to Cheek
50. Jimmy Somerville
51. Boughs of Holly
52. Starship
53. Country Music
54. Cathy Dennis
55. Kraftwerk
56. Miles Davis
57. Mötley Crüe
58. New Order
59. I Love Rock 'n' Roll
60. Violin
61. Some Might Say
62. Claudio Monteverdi
63. Four
64. Bananarama
65. Duran Duran
66. Rubato
67. The Rolling Stones
68. Kylie Minogue
69. Billy-Ray
70. Counterpoint
71. Shostakovich
72. Dizzy Gillespie
73. Wannabe
74. The Sound of Music
75. Bob Dylan
76. Yazoo
77. Scarecrow
78. Verdi
79. Adagio
80. Manchester
81. Cornet
82. Italy
83. 1956
84. Big Band
85. Dennis Wilson
86. Richard Strauss
87. Crunk
88. Xylophone
89. Snow White
90. AC/DC
91. Drums
92. The Kinks
93. Helen Shapiro
94. At Monte Carlo
95. Nadine Coyle
96. Triad
97. Igor
98. Mark Owen
99. 4
100. 1986

GENERAL KNOWLEDGE

1. Mullet
2. Retriever
3. Capricorn
4. Gorilla
5. The Hague
6. Angela Lansbury
7. Foreign Secretary
8. Andropov
9. Bros
10. 7
11. Crash
12. Italy
13. Archaeology
14. Molière
15. Lambeth Palace
16. 1974
17. Coyote
18. Sicily
19. Geese
20. Benny
21. A Cocktail
22. Euphrates
23. 1970s
24. Shikoku
25. Monkey
26. California
27. Brace
28. South America
29. Bread
30. Walker
31. Tailoring
32. Africa
33. Warsaw
34. Hung Parliament
35. Kirkcaldy and Cowdenbeath
36. Fertile
37. Spanish
38. Ginger Rogers
39. Scroddled
40. The Coldstream Guards
41. Per Diem
42. Fighter Planes
43. Brazil
44. The Bends
45. New Delhi
46. Prince William
47. Tax Collector
48. Longfellow
49. Lemur
50. Heisei
51. Queen Victoria
52. Bismarck
53. By The Way
54. Childbirth
55. Knight
56. Magistrate
57. Rigoletto
58. Australia
59. Sett
60. Visual Art
61. Alkali Metals
62. George Bernard Shaw
63. Photographer
64. Drake
65. Rum
66. Psychiatrist
67. 1973
68. Tucson, Arizona
69. South Africa
70. Volkswagen
71. The Stage Curtains
72. Norway
73. Brigitte Bardot
74. Cantilever
75. A Room With a View
76. USA
77. Bertrand Russell
78. A Fan
79. Princess Anne
80. Music
81. Gloomy
82. Sperm Whale
83. No, No, Nanette
84. Dog
85. Daily
86. 1989
87. A Flax Plant
88. Spy
89. Perfume
90. Ray Winstone
91. Hair Washing
92. Müller
93. Jim Clark
94. Pottery
95. Fat Tuesday
96. Water Flea
97. Sunday
98. Lincolnshire
99. Oranges and Lemons
100. Conducting

1. Spain
2. 43 AD
3. Amelia Earhart
4. Lawman
5. Soviet Union
6. The Ruhr Valley
7. Charles I
8. Confederacy
9. Vikings
10. George III
11. The Battle of Britain
12. Greek
13. Speakeasies
14. Germany
15. Murmillo
16. Ethelbert
17. Cornwall
18. The Longbow
19. Turkey
20. MacArthur
21. Edward Murrow
22. Cunard
23. 11th
24. Hadrian
25. 1991
26. Argentina
27. 68
28. Sheffield
29. 18th
30. Buffalo Bill
31. Edward IV
32. Purple
33. The Vikings
34. The Phalanx
35. 1612
36. The Boer Wars
37. Great Soul
38. Hawker
39. Canada
40. Zambia
41. Ambassador Hotel
42. Plymouth
43. Malta
44. Roger II
45. Neutral
46. English Civil War
47. Ferdinand de Lesseps
48. Throat
49. Agriculture
50. Navvies

51. Jane Seymour
52. Horatio
53. Bailey
54. Medicine
55. Venice
56. Judah
57. Airship
58. Road Building
59. Joan of Arc
60. SS Montrose
61. Indian Mutiny
62. Thomas Edison
63. River Tees
64. Europe
65. Alfonso d'Este
66. Ottoman
67. Nosey
68. Tank
69. Italy
70. Elizabeth I
71. Assyrian
72. St Paul's Cathedral
73. Pharoahs
74. The Colosseum
75. Ferdinand Magellan
76. Soviet Union
77. Crassus
78. 19th
79. Puritanism
80. HMS Victory
81. Boy Scouts
82. Beadle
83. The Battle of Salerno
84. The Gask Ridge
85. Body Armour
86. Highwayman
87. Brown Bess
88. Hadrian
89. Hacksilver
90. Russia
91. The Arabian Peninsula
92. Franklin D. Roosevelt
93. Mussolini
94. Lions
95. Poor Laws
96. Bayeux Tapestry
97. Senatorial
98. Louis XV
99. Bicycle
100. David Maxwell Fyfe

1. Chris Evans
2. Sanskrit
3. Bristol
4. Paisley
5. Max Mirnyi
6. Jaws
7. Sabre
8. Folly
9. ABC
10. Ceramics
11. Dragon's Teeth
12. Albert
13. The Phantom of the Opera
14. Miss Otis
15. Descartes
16. Buddleia
17. Red Tape
18. Western
19. Moose
20. Julius Caesar
21. Punjab
22. 2001
23. Session
24. Judaism
25. Beef
26. 1940s
27. The Housemartins
28. Bolas Spider
29. Cheese
30. Genoa
31. Australian Alps
32. Alcatraz
33. Financière
34. Portugal
35. Ramblers' Association
36. Annapolis
37. Names
38. Euripides
39. Norma
40. Teeth
41. Grange Hill
42. Cross of St Andrew
43. Zara Phillips
44. Tortoise
45. Diana Vickers
46. The Good
47. Firth of Clyde
48. Kayak
49. Cairo
50. Bassoon

51. Jamboree
52. Superman
53. Tube Alloys
54. Ancona
55. Conducting
56. Raise the Anchor
57. 1983
58. Miller's Crossing
59. 87
60. The Grateful Dead
61. Noël Coward
62. Elizabeth Bennet
63. Crow's Nest
64. Elton John
65. Stomach
66. Desperate Dan
67. Contempt
68. The Grand Tour
69. Arctic
70. Scotland
71. Malta
72. Nicole Appleton
73. 1980
74. Six Days
75. Housewife
76. Newgate
77. Bob Geldof
78. Lina Wertmuller
79. 1989
80. Kakistocracy
81. Loyd Grossman
82. 3
83. Neverland
84. Ray Winstone
85. By the Grace of God
86. Sight
87. Cryptology
88. Sleep
89. Valkyries
90. Distilling
91. Stock Exchange
92. Stymie
93. Printing
94. Grits
95. Fish
96. Sloane Square
97. Solitaire
98. Jack Cohen
99. Spain
100. Dionysus

1. Apple
2. Old Vic
3. The Decameron
4. Paul Cézanne
5. Strindberg
6. Oran
7. Wash
8. William Shakespeare
9. Chief Bromden
10. Ingres
11. English Civil Wars
12. Gertrude Stein
13. Medical Examiner
14. Bolton Wanderers
15. Bentley Drummle
16. Gus
17. Dover
18. Simon Pegg
19. St Clare's
20. The Two Gentlemen of Verona
21. Susan Philipsz
22. Three Sisters
23. Dawn French
24. Erich Maria Remarque
25. The Wombles
26. Suits
27. Gilded Bronze
28. Gyles Brandreth
29. Nottingham
30. The Man of Mode
31. 15th Century
32. Painter
33. Martina Cole
34. New Moon
35. Justin Bieber
36. Modigliani
37. 4
38. W.B. Yeats
39. Sophie Kinsella
40. Writing Poetry
41. Green
42. David Copperfield
43. James Herriot
44. George Bernard Shaw
45. Private Detective
46. Descender
47. Elizabeth Siddal
48. Wood
49. Black Beauty
50. Australia

51. King Lear
52. Along Came a Spider
53. Roman
54. Patrick Leigh Fermor
55. Miss Marple
56. Who Moved My Cheese?
57. Philip Larkin
58. Rent Collector
59. World War I
60. Hunt
61. Eric Gill
62. Dogs
63. H.G. Wells
64. On the Bummel
65. Painting
66. Jan Van Eyck
67. His Hand
68. Tarzan of the Apes
69. March Hare
70. India
71. Bisque
72. Piccolo
73. Seamus Heaney
74. English National Opera
75. Kate Mosse
76. Majorca
77. Tennyson
78. Dr Seuss
79. Piano
80. Ballet
81. Smetana
82. St Crispin
83. Ted Hughes
84. John Fowles
85. Beethoven
86. A Golden Ticket
87. Hans Christian Andersen
88. Pablo Picasso
89. Virgil
90. Ents
91. Aaron Copland
92. Inspector Wexford
93. John Everett Millais
94. Parody
95. Arpeggio
96. Lewis Carroll
97. Peter Mayle
98. Japan
99. Gone With the Wind
100. Willy Lott

1. Long Live the Queen
2. Fleas
3. Calabria
4. Alexandra
5. Myrmidons
6. Ruby Keeler
7. Edward H. Baily
8. Poland
9. California
10. Beer
11. Forget-Me-Not
12. Gin
13. Calaf
14. The Compleat Angler
15. Israel and Egypt
16. Co-operation
17. Diners Club
18. Military
19. New Forest
20. Zeus
21. Gerald Ford
22. Face
23. West Germany
24. Facebook
25. Han Solo
26. Speed Camera
27. Croatia
28. Geena Davis
29. South Korea
30. Rolls Royce
31. Elvis Presley
32. As You Like It
33. Chicago
34. Sailor
35. Augustus
36. German Shepherd
37. Aramaic
38. 13
39. Bergamo
40. Canterbury
41. Pressure
42. Winnie-the-Pooh
43. Judaism
44. Fish
45. Richard III
46. George Washington
47. Shtick
48. Lingua Franca
49. Porcelain
50. Anchor Cable
51. Submarines
52. White Horses
53. Idiot
54. Mutant Rat
55. Ferrari
56. Sony
57. Spain
58. Samaritans
59. Simon of Cyrene
60. Germany
61. Tail
62. Tupperware
63. Spitting Image
64. Infanta
65. Haifa
66. 8
67. Universities
68. Sledge
69. Hungary
70. Sea
71. India
72. Powder Monkey
73. Today
74. Robert Downey Jnr
75. Prawns
76. Snooker
77. Ninja
78. Turtle
79. Tracey Temple
80. Illinois
81. Danish
82. Submarine
83. Eat
84. Rebecca
85. Mozambique
86. Glassblowing
87. Head
88. Garfield
89. Aberdeen
90. James Bond
91. Ceiling
92. Robert Harris
93. Golden Horn
94. Chennai
95. Adkins
96. 1955
97. Lambada
98. Cloth
99. Oliver Hardy
100. Danny Blanchflower

1. Wales
2. Baseball
3. Cuba
4. Jack Beresford
5. Billie Jean King
6. Cricket
7. 1998
8. Twickenham
9. Carving
10. Louis Smith
11. LTA
12. Football
13. Spain
14. Hook
15. London
16. Formula 1
17. Wales
18. Ringette
19. Clinch
20. Starting Price
21. Monaco
22. Hampshire
23. David O'Leary
24. Mike Catt
25. Ferrari
26. Goal Attack
27. Two
28. Howard Eastman
29. Liverpool
30. Grey
31. South Africa
32. Weightlifting
33. Italian
34. Darts
35. Skiing
36. 1927
37. Dolly
38. Israel
39. Catgut
40. £800m
41. France
42. Volley
43. Mary Peters
44. Skiing
45. 14th
46. Rugby Union
47. Tennis
48. White
49. West Ham United
50. Show Jumping
51. Soviet Union
52. Cricket
53. Featherweight
54. Sheffield Wednesday
55. 60 Metres
56. Cork
57. The Bledisloe Cup
58. Tennis
59. Jack Nicklaus
60. Arsenal
61. Second
62. Luge
63. 3 Feet
64. Derby County
65. Rowing
66. Kapil Dev
67. West Indies
68. Jonah Lomu
69. 1500m
70. Long Jump
71. LA Lakers
72. 9
73. Forty
74. Birmingham
75. Golf
76. Belgium
77. 40mm
78. Christine Truman
79. Table Tennis
80. Argentina
81. Snooker
82. 8 Yards
83. Spider
84. Cricket
85. Prince William
86. Swimming
87. Golf
88. José Mourinho
89. Rugby Union
90. Sri Lanka
91. Jackie Stewart
92. Kerry Packer
93. Spots
94. Trampolining
95. Darts
96. London 1908
97. Alfa Romeo
98. Super Heavyweight
99. Triple Jump
100. Korea

1. Elizabeth I
2. Salisbury Cathedral
3. Laertes
4. Prince Andrew
5. 1946
6. Jackets
7. British Museum
8. William I
9. Lark
10. Freudian Slip
11. Vienna
12. Winston Churchill
13. Wiltshire
14. Wales
15. Jackie Trent
16. Claque
17. Photography
18. Painter
19. Hervey Allen
20. Furness Abbey
21. Gordon Brown
22. Lady Gaga
23. Bristol
24. Optometrist
25. Sweden
26. Danny Kaye
27. Asia
28. Railway Station
29. Physiotherapists
30. Tin Can
31. 1960
32. 28
33. Sarcastic
34. Ceylon
35. No Trumps
36. Rooster
37. 6
38. Giraffe
39. 13
40. Henotheism
41. John Boehner
42. 1950
43. James
44. Pope John Paul II
45. Alexandra Burke
46. Mussels
47. Standards
48. Jennifer Lopez
49. NBC
50. Shirt

51. Lead
52. Saliva
53. Fruit Cake
54. Mike Hussey
55. Sheffield
56. Denzel Washington
57. Mountain
58. New Zealand
59. Innocent
60. Julius Caesar
61. Selwyn Lloyd
62. Rose
63. Pod
64. Switzerland
65. Squamata
66. Keith Richards
67. Philippines
68. Blue Book
69. Sandie Shaw
70. Matthew Arnold
71. Fauntleroy
72. Grapefruit
73. Slight
74. Baron
75. Peter the Great
76. Charles Darwin
77. Noel Clarke
78. Weekend World
79. Port
80. India
81. Wilhelm I
82. Chile
83. Bedivere
84. Bobby Robson
85. Alan Garner
86. Popcorn
87. Clive Anderson
88. Brussels Sprout
89. Michigan
90. Korean War
91. Switzerland
92. Katrina and the Waves
93. Day of Wrath
94. Dog
95. New York Red Bulls
96. Silver Surfer
97. George Bernard Shaw
98. Jeffrey Archer
99. Jura
100. 1920s

SCIENCE

1. Hydrogen
2. Andrology
3. Iberian Lynx
4. Hans Krebs
5. Florida Everglades
6. 3
7. Geometry
8. Skin
9. Bird
10. Rn
11. 2000
12. 165 years
13. Armadillo
14. Italy
15. 6
16. Local Group
17. Iron
18. Antibiotic
19. Kidneys
20. Lizard
21. Cygnus
22. Teeth
23. Myanmar Snub-Nosed
24. Corundum
25. Palaeozoic
26. White Noise
27. Falcon
28. Sea
29. Trinity
30. Zoonosis
31. Within the Earth
32. Charles Babbage
33. Yellow Dye
34. Egg Tooth
35. Microwave Oven
36. Shagreen
37. Primate
38. Eyeball
39. Pathogen
40. Blue
41. Triangle
42. Pain
43. As
44. Auricular Muscles
45. Googleplex
46. Lemur
47. Laurel
48. Brain
49. 7
50. Neutron Bomb

51. Eye
52. Ants
53. Heart
54. Pharmacology
55. Joule
56. Mole
57. 1,064
58. Apollo 16
59. Bristles
60. 96
61. Solid
62. Hip
63. Water
64. Peripheral
65. Metal
66. Glass
67. Beetles
68. Vitamin K1
69. 1
70. Arachnids
71. Apricot
72. Helium
73. Alan Shepard
74. Stephen Jay Gould
75. Africa and Asia
76. Memory
77. Cholesterol
78. Daniel Gabriel
79. Pressurised Steam
80. Orion's Belt
81. Skin
82. Carbohydrates
83. Trees
84. Horse
85. Head
86. Biodegradable
87. Leather
88. Tin
89. Neptune
90. Fish
91. Float to the Surface
92. Africa
93. Moon
94. Martin Ryle
95. Lead
96. Heat
97. Rainbow
98. Dark Red
99. Great Tit
100. Two

GENERAL KNOWLEDGE

1. Bruce Willis
2. Illinois
3. Brick Lane
4. Matisse
5. Castanets
6. Wilton
7. Sea
8. Mercutio
9. Dancer
10. Underwater
11. Professor
12. Go Dutch
13. Hermes
14. Manse
15. Woodland
16. Ian MacGregor
17. Dundee
18. Chile
19. Korean
20. Glastonbury
21. Lake District
22. Rotterdam
23. Philippines
24. William McKinley
25. Photography
26. Scotland
27. Paper Tiger
28. Ashram
29. Ionic
30. Billy Connolly
31. Labour
32. Printed Words
33. German
34. Buddy Holly
35. Bert
36. Salient
37. Limestone
38. Melbourne
39. Photographer
40. Thursday
41. Spam
42. Le Corbusier
43. To Complain
44. Gerard Manley Hopkins
45. Speaker's Chaplain
46. Ireland
47. Barley
48. Women's League of Health and Beauty
49. Northamptonshire
50. Birds
51. David Bowie
52. Batman
53. Netherlands
54. Juventus
55. Earth Day
56. Philadelphia
57. Dance
58. St Pancras
59. Alexander Pope
60. Zimbabwe
61. Robert Zemeckis
62. Netherlands
63. Thursday
64. 225
65. S
66. Bikini
67. Doctor
68. Sol
69. Karl Marx
70. The Medium
71. Heart of Darkness
72. Froth
73. USA
74. South Beach
75. Challah
76. Jean-Paul Sartre
77. She
78. Bilateral
79. Walter Greenwood
80. Afghanistan
81. Ramekin
82. Biplane
83. Judaism
84. Vertex
85. Window
86. V
87. Apple
88. Neneh Cherry
89. Mare's Tails
90. 4
91. Taylor Hackford
92. Judaism
93. Fame
94. Goalkeeper
95. Equality and Human Rights Commission
96. Portuguese Water Dog
97. Law
98. Doctor Foster
99. 1976
100. Cliff Richard

1. Extras
2. Hospital
3. Will Ferrell
4. David Schwimmer
5. Australia
6. Othello
7. Miss Matty Jenkyns
8. Ricky Tomlinson
9. Anthony Edwards
10. Jim Carrey
11. Emma Bunton
12. Blossom Avenue
13. Elvis Presley
14. Eiffel Tower
15. Michael Gambon
16. Jock
17. Tom Selleck
18. Cable
19. Tomorrow Never Dies
20. Plastics
21. Blackpool
22. Leslie Nielsen
23. Shrewsbury Abbey
24. Dynasty
25. Denton
26. Alain Delon
27. Peggy Mitchell
28. The X Factor
29. South America
30. Spike Jonze
31. 1981
32. 3-2-1
33. The Wizard of Oz
34. Goats
35. Michael Rodd
36. Gene Tierney
37. Bill Murray
38. Martina Hingis
39. The Wright Stuff
40. Rex Harrison
41. Chris Rock
42. Barney
43. Match of the Day
44. Peter Cook and Dudley Moore
45. Home Alone
46. Inspector Clouseau
47. John McEnroe
48. Hospital
49. Morgan Freeman
50. Neil

51. James Cameron
52. Frenzy
53. The Royle Family
54. James May
55. Kenneth Kendall
56. Friday the 13th
57. Lee Evans
58. Tony Robinson
59. The IT Crowd
60. A Nightmare on Elm Street
61. David
62. Tony Randall
63. Neighbours
64. Bruce Forsyth
65. Chris Noth
66. When Harry Met Sally
67. Robert De Niro
68. Desperate Romantics
69. Tony Hancock
70. Richard Attenborough
71. Star Trek: The Next Generation
72. Christopher Eccleston
73. John Hughes
74. Big Brother
75. Biopic
76. Woody Allen
77. Mice
78. ITV
79. Charlize Theron
80. EastEnders
81. Roger Livesey
82. The Rock
83. Bergerac
84. Jessica Rabbit
85. Walking Dogs
86. Japan
87. Oliver Postgate
88. Emma Thompson
89. Abbott and Costello
90. Fred Flintstone
91. Vietnam War
92. Alan Rickman
93. Alien
94. Edward G. Robinson
95. Paul Bettany
96. Blue Peter
97. Robert Lindsay
98. Herman Munster
99. The Golden Girls
100. Mark Ruffalo

1. Singing
2. Money
3. Prince Michael of Kent
4. Supergirl
5. Japan
6. Harpsichord
7. Every Two Years
8. Pisces
9. Gangway
10. Economics
11. Opal
12. Hilda Ogden
13. The Tortoise and the Hare
14. Italian
15. New Orleans
16. Madeira
17. Trees
18. London
19. Marathon
20. Jetsam
21. Cameroon
22. Runic Alphabet
23. Netherlands
24. Kettling
25. The Exorcist
26. Town Hall
27. Corolla
28. Crossbow
29. Typeface
30. Hare
31. Lord Lieutenant
32. Rear-Admiral
33. Philip K. Dick
34. Giant Panda
35. King
36. Cowboy
37. Butterfly
38. Taio Cruz
39. Red
40. Spinach
41. Thames
42. Film
43. David Bowie
44. Norman Wisdom
45. Damned
46. Old Stoics
47. Full Metal Jacket
48. North Korea
49. Airport
50. Bird
51. Julie Walters
52. Los Angeles
53. Sinead O'Connor
54. Escapement
55. Women
56. Pommel
57. Excelling
58. Ambrose Phillips
59. Jean-Paul Sartre
60. USA
61. Terry Wogan
62. Tasmania
63. Alexei Leonov
64. Frogs and Toads
65. Jacob Zuma
66. E
67. Norway
68. Judd Apatow
69. Eyes
70. 1970s
71. Passant
72. New York
73. Linen
74. Intensive
75. Artist
76. Pembrokeshire
77. The Shipping News
78. Turban
79. Drama
80. South Africa
81. Drums
82. Dumbarton
83. Logan Stone
84. Reginald Pole
85. Hans Christian Andersen
86. Swimming
87. Snakes
88. Thomas Jefferson
89. Bernard Cornwell
90. Bahrain
91. Trousers
92. Chris Hollins
93. Liam Gallagher
94. Dundee
95. Longleat
96. Tree
97. Cards
98. Rolls and Royce
99. Cookery
100. Crema

1. York
2. Atlantic
3. California
4. Green and White
5. Ecuador
6. Afghanistan
7. Pacific
8. Denmark
9. Oregon
10. Euro
11. Indian
12. France
13. Northern Cape
14. Guyana
15. North Yorkshire
16. Atlantic Ocean
17. Ranker
18. Yardang
19. Washington
20. Thames
21. India
22. South Downs
23. Rennes
24. Slovenia
25. Israel
26. Pacific
27. Shetland
28. Newcastle Upon Tyne
29. Afghanistan
30. Italy
31. Adriatic Sea
32. 274
33. Kent
34. Karakorum
35. Australia
36. Netherlands
37. Louisiana
38. Hesse
39. Corsica
40. Mountain
41. Loire
42. Christchurch
43. Cumbria
44. Manila
45. Arctic
46. 5
47. Skegness
48. Ubac
49. Mediterranean Sea
50. Belize Dollar

51. Michigan
52. North York Moors
53. Switzerland
54. Essex
55. Pacific
56. Mount Lofty Ranges
57. Durban
58. Selsey Bill
59. Frankfurt
60. Philippines
61. Linlithgow
62. Rockies
63. Greece
64. Green
65. 4,000 miles
66. Marseille
67. Maputo
68. Euro
69. 62 Million
70. Sydney
71. 893
72. Persian Gulf
73. Peak District
74. Black and Red
75. City
76. 6
77. Lake Lucerne
78. Australia
79. Atlantic
80. Plug
81. Devon
82. Nelson River
83. Goa
84. Sahara
85. Dolomites
86. East Sussex
87. 3 Million
88. Cardiff
89. Guilder
90. Costa del Sol
91. Saskatchewan
92. Venice of the East
93. Southampton
94. Blackpool
95. 9 Million
96. Great Dividing Range
97. Johannesburg
98. Dorset
99. Abu Dhabi
100. Ibiza

1. En Garde
2. Wales
3. Hills of Rome
4. Mashed Potato and Cheese
5. Pig
6. Codicil
7. Banns
8. Boston Baked Beans
9. Loyd Grossman
10. Queensland
11. Caria
12. Bigfoot
13. Stallion
14. Spring
15. Mad About You
16. Camberwell Beauty
17. Chin
18. Palace of Versailles
19. Greenish-blue
20. Assumption
21. Dance Step
22. Claude Chabrol
23. Four-O'Clock Family
24. Australia
25. Beautiful
26. Wardrobe
27. Mustard
28. Florence
29. Turkey
30. Singapore Sling
31. Gérard Houllier
32. Piccadilly
33. Peter Ustinov
34. Socrates
35. Arctic
36. Obadiah
37. Dog
38. The xx
39. John Major
40. Cormac Murphy-O'Connor
41. Comedy
42. Tin Lizzie
43. Tony Benn
44. Australia
45. Nigeria
46. Helen
47. Restaurants
48. John Henry Newman
49. Ethiopia
50. Anthony Hopkins

51. Boris Bikes
52. Lynda Carter
53. New Zealand
54. Doughnuts
55. The Guardian
56. At the Front
57. Twill
58. Wallace and Gromit
59. Army
60. Stringed Instrument
61. Chicago Bears
62. The Prisoner
63. Oysters
64. Rebus
65. Cliveden Set
66. Merlot
67. West Ham United
68. James
69. Bricklayer
70. Heracles
71. Dalai Lama
72. Ambrose Bierce
73. Chaos
74. Mother Teresa
75. Canada
76. Black Pig's Dyke
77. Chile
78. Horses
79. Cookery
80. Robert De Niro
81. Antoine de Saint-Exupéry
82. Yucca
83. Curry
84. Fashion
85. Chile
86. Hamlet
87. Horse
88. Gnarls Barkley
89. Euro 96
90. FBI
91. Knife
92. Dot Dash
93. Shepherd's Pie
94. Edward Heath
95. Gladioli
96. International Orange
97. Frisbee
98. Cherry
99. Chess
100. Pear

1. Big Foot
2. 38
3. Danny DeVito
4. The Pig
5. Solomon Islands
6. Florin
7. Marcel Cerdan
8. Super Furry Animals
9. W.B. Yeats
10. Le Pont De La Tour
11. Fakie
12. W.B. Yeats
13. 7 metres
14. Christy Turlington
15. North America
16. Aesop
17. Board Game
18. Vienna
19. Ambidextrous
20. Mr Fantastic
21. Brian Paddick
22. Last Monday in May
23. Fringe
24. Bicycle
25. David Shrigley
26. India
27. The Mayor of Casterbridge
28. Poet
29. Fish
30. Auckland
31. Thick Noodles
32. Mashed Potato and Cheese
33. Heartbreak House
34. Innocent
35. Sooty
36. Venice
37. Barry Norman
38. P
39. Molière
40. X
41. Sybil Thorndike
42. HMS Bulwark
43. Thailand
44. Plane
45. Roll Deep
46. Rupert Everett
47. Sweden
48. Gianfranco Ferré
49. William Beveridge (author of the Beveridge Report)
50. Boca Juniors (acc. Boca)
51. India
52. Abbey Clancy
53. Single
54. El Salvador
55. St Paul's Cathedral
56. Buddy's Song
57. Ian Messiter
58. Margaret Thatcher
59. Indonesia
60. China
61. Arsenal
62. Shiva
63. Obverse
64. Bob Holness
65. Billy Elliot
66. Printer
67. Agenda
68. Hindi
69. The Orkneys
70. The Shmoo
71. Crinoline
72. Modern Review
73. Magna Carta
74. Quoits
75. Canada

ACKNOWLEDGEMENTS

On the 10th of November 2003 *Eggheads* was born, and what better way to mark our 10th anniversary than with a fabulous quiz book.

I'd like to take this opportunity to thank some of the people who have contributed to the success of *Eggheads* over the years.

Dermot Murnaghan and Jeremy Vine for not only being top quiz masters but for also being two of the nicest people you could ever hope to work with.

The Eggheads themselves for the stoic defence of their quizzing reputation. No matter what questions get thrown at them they continue to astound me with their knowledge.

Everyone at the BBC who continues to support the programme so enthusiastically, with special thanks to Jo Street.

Thanks to all the production teams, editors and crew who have worked so so hard on the show over the years – in particular Nick Pagan, Jo Dean and the rest of their question team for the thousands of fascinating questions they've written, Suzanne Pearse for directing nearly every episode so wonderfully, Jane Myers whose brilliance as a script supervisor makes my job so much easier and finally Katy Smith for managing the production so effortlessly. All the folks at Editworks and especially Tim Mills for brilliantly editing hundreds of episodes. I'd also like to say a personal thank you to Andy Culpin, *Eggheads* Executive Producer since day one, for not only giving me the opportunity to work on the show, for which I will be eternally grateful, but for also sharing my passion for this wonderful programme.

To the extremely talented people who set the bar so high during their time producing the programme: Andrew Musson, Eileen Herlihy and Tessa McHugh.

Thank you to Briony Gowlett at Simon & Schuster and Shirley Patton at ITV for getting the book up and running in the first place.

A mention to Susie Hall for compiling all the questions you're about to read and for putting up with me continually changing things.

A special thank you to all the teams who have attempted to defeat the Eggheads despite the obvious difficulties this entails.

My thanks to the viewers for their loyalty and quizzing passion. I hope they can continue to enjoy their show for a long time to come.

And, finally, thanks to you for buying this book. A lot of thought has gone into its creation and hopefully you will enjoy testing yourself, your friends and your family against the same questions that the Eggheads have faced and who knows, if you learn every answer contained in these pages; all the capitals of the world; every element in the Periodic Table and the name of every king and queen, the dates of their reigns and their shoe sizes then maybe, just maybe, one day you too could be any Egghead, maybe . . .

Robert Dean, Series Editor